COUNTRY
WOODWORKER

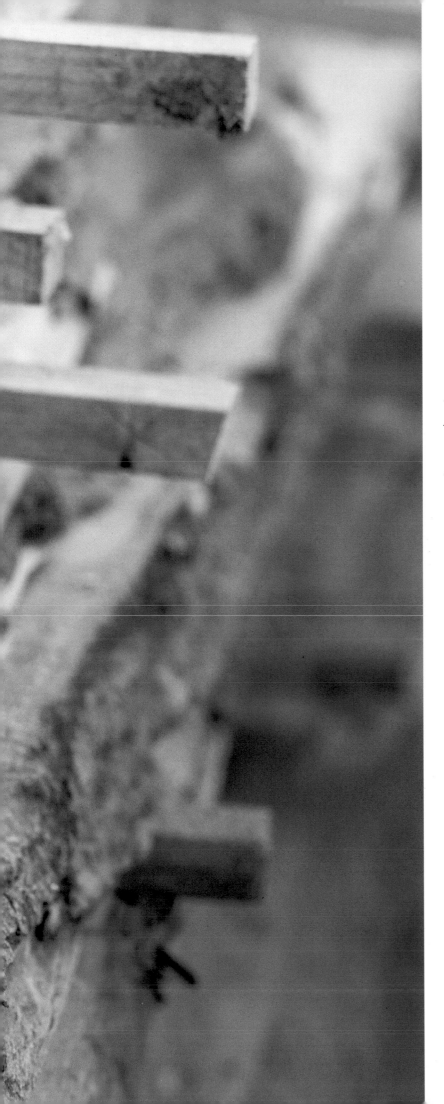

COUNTRY
WOODWORKER

Jack Hill

photography by James Merrell

MITCHELL BEAZLEY

First published in Great Britain in 1995
by Mitchell Beazley
an imprint of Reed Consumer Books Limited
Michelin House, 81 Fulham Road
London SW3 6RB
and Auckland, Melbourne, Singapore and Toronto

Text and projects © Jack Hill 1995
Illustrations © Reed International Books Limited 1995
Reprinted 1996

Senior Art Editor **Larraine Shamwana**
Senior Editor **Jennifer Jones**
Designer **Geoff Fennell**
Editors **Jonathan Hilton, Maggi McCormick**
Production **Michelle Thomas**
Illustrator **Julie Douglas**

Art Director **Jacqui Small**
Executive Editor **Judith More**

A CIP record for this book is available from the British Library

ISBN 1 85732 390 4

The publishers have made every effort to ensure that all instructions
given in this book are accurate and safe, but they cannot accept
liability for any resulting injury, damage or loss to either person or
property whether direct or consequential and howsoever arising. The
author and publishers will be grateful for any information which will
assist them in keeping future editions up to date.

Typeset in Monotype Sabon 10/15pt

Origination by Mandarin Singapore
Produced by Mandarin Offset
Printed and bound in China

CONTENTS

Living with Wood

Wood is the most used of all our natural resources. Like food, wood has sustained humanity's basic needs since earliest times. Early cultures are dated by the materials used in axe-making – the Stone, Bronze, and Iron Ages – tools developed for cutting wood and as weapons of war. Together, wood and the axe provided early mankind with fuel for fire and, later, with shelter, too.

EVOLVING SKILLS AND TECHNIQUES
Throughout the ancient world, in Egypt, across Asia, and in Europe and the Americas, wood was used for buildings, furniture making, and a host of domestic ware and agricultural implements. Workers in wood came to recognize the different properties of various trees and so developed techniques for using them more advantageously. Medieval artisans learned how to cut, shape, carve, and, above all, how to make joints. Although their early efforts produced simple joints, they were solidly made – so much so that some examples have lasted until the present day. Throughout this period, new tools and working methods were evolving and, in due course, furniture and artifacts made by craftsmen in the cities were eventually to reach a high level of sophistication.

In the countryside, however, village woodworkers – often using the simple axe, adze, and auger – continued to make pieces of furniture in a plainer style. These pieces catered to the requirements of a rural people more interested in function than in fashion. The trees that provided the raw material for these enterprises were in abundant supply locally and, as more of the world was explored by the European seafaring nations, trees – both familiar species as well as new ones – were found to be widespread and even more plentiful. And since trees grow and can thus be cultivated, it was eventually recognized that trees could potentially provide a constant supply of useful material, and so become a renewable resource – a fact that is still not universally appreciated even today.

Experience soon showed that the wood from one tree was better than that from another for specific applications. Ash, for example, is extremely strong yet elastic, well able to withstand hard shocks, and so it was used extensively in making handles for tools. Oak – once a plentiful source of wood – is both strong and hard and its heart wood is extremely durable. It is also quite a heavy wood. Oak was used widely in building work and furniture making.

THE COLONIAL ERA
When exploration gave way to colonization, the early settlers in the New World found trees with similar characteristics and properties to those that grew in their native lands: they discovered new ones, too, some with very different properties. Trees were everywhere, and they first had to be felled to make way for settlements and to provide cleared land for crops. The process of land clearance for cultivation produced masses of timber for building and firewood. Once more, basic needs of food, shelter, and fuel were to be satisfied, and the most useful tool proved yet again to be the axe.

There is no doubt that the thought uppermost in the minds of those early colonists was simple survival. What they did first was what was needed most, and when it came to furniture-making the same priorities applied. A table, stools, bed, and perhaps a chair or cradle, a chest or cupboard for storage, and a few kitchen utensils – little else was actually needed.

Left - ALL THE INGREDIENTS OF THE COUNTRY STYLE ARE BROUGHT TOGETHER HERE – LIMEWASHED, BARE STONE WALLS, PLAIN FLOORBOARDS AND EXPOSED WOODEN BEAMS. THE TABLE AND CHAIRS ARE INSPIRED BY THE WORK OF THE SHAKERS. DRYING HERBS AND HANGING BASKETS COMPLETE THE LOOK.

Above - THIS STURDY "STABLE DOOR" WITH ITS WROUGHT IRON ATTACHMENTS IS A FITTING EXAMPLE OF THE COLLABORATIVE WORK OF WOODWORKER AND BLACKSMITH. ORIGINAL DOORS SUCH AS THIS ARE NOW QUITE RARE DUE TO THE RAVAGES OF "RESTORERS" AND THE FASHION FOR REPLACING OLD WITH NEW.

A RETURN TO BASICS

Although there was wood to be found in abundance, there were few tools with which to work it. As a result, the first utensils and pieces of furniture were very plain and severely functional. Those who made it, familiar as they might well have been with the more sophisticated styles of contemporary European tastes, were by the nature of their circumstances obliged to adopt the more simple, rural tradition of working wood – a style typical of an English, Dutch, or Scandinavian village carpenter. In spite of evidence that there were skilled craftsmen among the early settlers, they returned purposely to the work and working methods of the country woodworker, using their ingenuity and skills to make the best of what they had and what they knew.

These pioneer woodworkers used solid-wood construction and, because nails and screws were difficult to obtain and glue virtually unheard of, they used dovetail and dado joints and pegged or wedged their mortise and tenons, just as their European counterparts had done for thousands of years.

Inevitably, colonists from the different countries that settled in the Americas brought with them their own traditions, and these were to have an impact on local furniture making, as did the contribution of some religious communities, such as the Shakers and the Amish. New England, Spanish and Dutch Colonial, Pennsylvania German, French, Scandinavian, are all representative of what we now call American "country" furniture. In Europe, the different countries retained their individual styles, and even within countries regional variations existed and exist still. The wide range of styles in painted furniture to be found in the European continent is a good example of this rich diversity.

AN APPRECIATION OF COUNTRY STYLE

Today, what was made in the village workshops of 18th- and 19th-century Europe and in the backwoods and early settlements of colonial America, is highly regarded on account of its simple beauty and stark utility. It has come to epitomize a particular time and way of life, a time when things were more natural and the pace more relaxed than it is today in our technology-driven world. Country woodwork, perhaps more than anything else, is central to the so-called country style; the very essence of country living.

Yet "country" is more than just a style, much more than simply a fashion or a fad. Rather, it is of enduring interest, a rich treasury of ideas and images, a heritage of past practices and traditions, something timeless in its simplicity. It was a style born out of necessity to people grateful merely to survive, unpretentious yet independently creative. In their self-sufficiency and in their adaptability, these craftsmen relied solely on traditional skills, limited tools, and the availability of natural resources.

The two-fold purpose of this book is to show you how the furniture and wooden artefacts of these bygone ages can contribute towards a country style of living, and, in a very practical way, to provide the means of achieving this objective. The inspirational pages that open each new section are packed with exciting design ideas for creating a whole country look; the practical projects that follow encourage you to make your own hand-crafted pieces, which, in time, may become heirlooms in their own right, cherished by later generations. Living with wood is undeniably pleasurable and working with wood can be deeply satisfying and rewarding. Here, within, these pages, is all you need to know to become a country woodworker.

Above - SUNSHINE SHINING THROUGH A WOVEN SCREEN DAPPLES THE SEAT OF THIS RATHER UNUSUAL CHAIR. IT IS A FAIRLY MODERN PIECE, AND ITS DESIGN IS BASED ON A STYLE FOUND IN PARTS OF RURAL IRELAND WHERE IT IS USUALLY KNOWN AS A SLIGO CHAIR.

Right - THE CORNER OF THIS COUNTRY KITCHEN SHOWS A MIXTURE OF OLD AND NEW. THE MODERN KITCHEN RANGE TO THE LEFT OF THE DOOR IS FLANKED BY A SIMPLE CUPBOARD LADEN WITH COLOURFUL CONTAINERS AND WOODEN BOWLS DATING FROM THE 19TH CENTURY.

Living Rooms

There is a clear line of descent from the original rural cottage, where families once lived, ate, and sometimes slept crowded together into a single room, to today's modern country living room. Generations ago, the one-room rural cottage and its hearth was the centre of all domestic activity and, no less today, the living room remains a focal point and gathering place for family and friends. Where once its furnishings and decoration were determined by basic necessities, the essential ingredients of the living room now are comfort and relaxation. With perhaps the exception of the kitchen (see pages 72-85), it provides the least private, yet the most homely, room in the house. It is, in the strictly literal sense, a room for living in.

EARLIER TIMES REMEMBERED

The average rural family room of earlier times was a simple affair, and even by the 19th century most families who lived off the land made do with the barest minimum of furniture and enjoyed few creature comforts. But wherever a cottager or small farmer was a little more prosperous there was a discernible element of coziness. Here is how the social historian and novelist Flora Thompson describes English cottages of the 1880s: "In nearly all the cottages there was but one room downstairs, and many of these were poor and bare, with only a table and a few chairs and stools for furniture and a superannuated potato-sack thrown down by way of a hearthrug. Other rooms (in other cottages) were bright and cosy with dressers of crockery, cushioned chairs, pictures on the wall and brightly coloured hand-made rag rugs on the floor. In these there would be pots of geraniums, fuchsias and old-fashioned, sweet smelling musk on the window sills. In the older cottages there were grandfather clocks, gate legged tables and rows of pewter . . ." (*Lark Rise to Candleford*, 1945.)

THE ELEMENTS OF COUNTRY STYLE

It is the descriptive atmosphere of rural coziness from the likes of Flora Thompson that should be your guide in creating a true country style in today's family living room. Starting with the basics, paint walls, whether plastered or wood-boarded, in country colours such as cream, soft blues, greens or pinks. Plastered walls can also be wallpapered – for patterns, choose simple stripes or miniprints with naturalistic motifs such as acorn and leaf. Soft furnishings should also reinforce the country theme. Fabrics for curtains can be plain, striped, checked or, for prettiness, a traditional chintz. Combine these with checks and stripes in natural fabrics, such as cotton and linen and linen blends for chair and settee covers. Woven blankets and hand-stitched quilts complement the rugged texture of the wood and add both colour and comfort. Use them as throws over armchairs and settees or as wallhangings.

When it comes to the furniture nothing should be too perfect, too precious, or too highly polished. No matching sets of chairs and no "fitted furniture". For this is not the equivalent of the drawing room of more opulent households, or the descendant of the Victorian parlour. Furniture should be functional without being too formal, durable without being too utilitarian. And wood – its textural surface quality and hand-worked mellow tones in perfect harmony with the simple, homely ambience – is, of course, the ideal material to create this mood and purpose.

The room itself needs to be carefully studied, since it may have much to contribute to the desired atmosphere. Wood is often the feature of wall construction, either as part or all of its structure, or it can be applied as panelling. Original, exposed wooden beams, kept natural and not painted, are in many instances central to the country

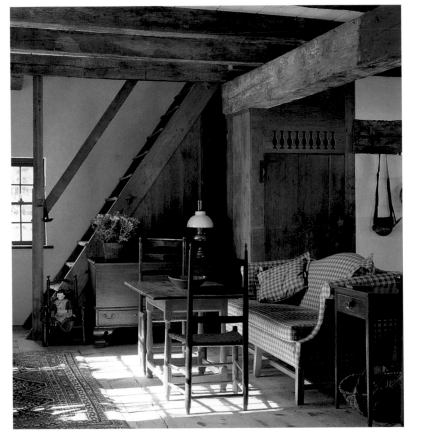

Above - FROM THE HEAVY CEILING BEAMS TO THE LIGHTWEIGHT LADDERBACK CHAIRS, THE VERSATILITY OF WOOD IN A RURAL SETTING IS CLEARLY DEMONSTRATED. THE PINE TABLE AND THE CHAIRS ARE FROM THE SHENANDOAH VALLEY IN VIRGINIA, THE SOFA IS IN THE COUNTRY CHIPPENDALE STYLE.

Right - THE FIREPLACE IS OFTEN THE FOCUS OF A ROOM, AND PARTICULARLY SO IN A LIVING ROOM, WHERE, AS HERE, THE MOST COMFORTABLE SEATING NATURALLY FINDS A PLACE AROUND IT. WOVEN AND QUILTED TEXTILES PROVIDE BRIGHT SPLASHES OF COLOUR AND WARMTH.

The hearth has always been a special place in the home, and it still is. An open fire, with brightly burning logs and the tangy smell of wood smoke, evokes primitive senses in us, and perhaps cherished memories, too, while its flickering light casts mysterious shadows and an elusive glow around the room, reflecting back from polished surfaces or people's faces. Where an open fire is impracticable for some reason, consider using the space for an alternative source of heat, such as a cast-iron woodburning stove or a modern gas-fired equivalent.

Around the fire are to be found the most comfortable chairs in the house. These are an invitation to sit and savour the delights of the time and place; a subtle suggestion that you have done enough for the day and now should pause and take time for yourself. For children, low stools will keep them close to the fire's glow. For adults, choose a sturdy Windsor – a comfortable design despite its rigidly woody appearance – or an upholstered chair, for both are equally at home by the hearth. And here, as elsewhere, the outdoor look of the Adirondack style of rustic furniture blends well into this informal setting. These pieces, which are made from wood that is rough-hewn and untreated, bring with them into the home the feel not just of the wood but of the forest itself.

THE SEARCH FOR COMFORT

When the concept of comfort in the home came to be a subject of serious consideration, sometime in the 16th century, it was usually related to the source of heat in a room. That, and the avoidance of draughts. Central-heating systems, insulation, and draught-proofing tend to solve the problem today, but in these earlier times it was the furniture makers who provided at least the partial answer – the high-backed settle.

Illustrations of 17th-century inns and cosy, comfortable cottage interiors frequently depict deep, warm fireplaces flanked by a settle or, more often, a pair of settles, one on either side. When used in this fashion, an enclosed space is formed separate from the rest of the room, combining fireside seating for several people with adequate protection from the ever-present menace of draughts.

A true country piece of furniture, the settle was never accepted into the fashionable drawing rooms of the affluent – not, that is, until it had altered its shape and acquired an upholstered form, to be reborn as the settee. It is said that the settle is a development of the chest, which had always invited use as a seat, along with its other function as a box-like storage container. Adding a back and arms to a chest easily produces the box settle, which is the proper name given to those pieces that incorporate a lidded storage space below the seat. An added refinement came in the form of draught-excluding end pieces – these shaped head-protection pieces were later adopted in the design of the still-popular wing armchair.

Above - THE SIMPLE CONSTRUCTION OF THIS TWO-TIER CUPBOARD OR DRESSER IN PAINTED YELLOW PINE IS TYPICAL OF THE EARLY NEW ENGLAND STYLE. A WELL-MADE, UNPRETENTIOUS COUNTRY PIECE, IT LOOKS AT HOME IN ANY ROOM IN THE HOUSE WHILE PROVIDING MUCH-NEEDED STORAGE SPACE.

Right - SETTLES WERE ORIGINALLY BUILT INTO THE FABRIC OF THE WALL, BUT BY THE END OF THE 16TH CENTURY THEY WERE FREESTANDING AND HAD MOVED CLOSER TO THE FIREPLACE. THIS LOVELY SETTLE IS A FINE EXAMPLE OF AN EARLY 18TH-CENTURY "BACON SETTLE" – SO-CALLED BECAUSE THE CUPBOARD IN THE FRAMED PANEL BACK PROVIDED SPACE FOR HANGING A SIDE OF BACON. THE SEAT LIFTS UP TO REVEAL A BOX FOR STORAGE.

cottage look. Beams give a room character and strength. They speak for the structure of the whole building and of the work of nameless village carpenters or pioneer woodsmen of long ago, the marks left by their simple tools their only epitaph.

The focus of this family room is the fireplace – the hearth, once the main, or perhaps the only, source of warmth and light. The fireplace may be of the open "inglenook" variety, deep enough and high enough to walk into, topped with a massive, smoke-blackened beam of oak or elm. Or it may be smaller and a little lower, with a mantel shelf above for displaying ornaments and family memorabilia.

Adapting a basic design

Resourceful woodworkers have adapted the settle, more than any other piece of furniture, to a number of ingenious, multipurpose functions. By having a back that folded over on hinges, it was made to convert into a useful table. This design was popular both in Europe and in colonial America, where it was usually made of pine. The usual modern name for this type of converting settle-table is monks' bench, a name which is probably erroneous, since they are more closely associated with wayside inns than with monasteries.

In some places, especially where space was limited, the settle-bed was popular. Acting as a long seat by day, its bottom portion could be opened out at night to provide a comfortable box bed. When they were not in use for sleeping purposes, the mattress and bed clothes could be conveniently stored inside out of the way. Parallels with the modern bed-settee are obvious. One other use of the settle – one that has, fortunately, not carried over to the present day – was the use of the lower part as a coop to house a laying hen or goose.

Many high-backed settles, like the one shown below, had cupboards in the back in which sides of bacon were hung, presumably to cure. Such cupboards – and others, both floor-standing and wall-hung and used for food storage – were once very common and are the ancestors of many, much grander, cabinets and cupboards used for a wide variety of different purposes today.

The name cupboard derives from the medieval "cup-borde", literally a board for storing cups or drinking vessels, often arranged in tiers with one board above another, in a fashion similar to what we now simply call shelves. In the Middle Ages, a closer equivalent to the modern cupboard was the English "aumbry" or the French

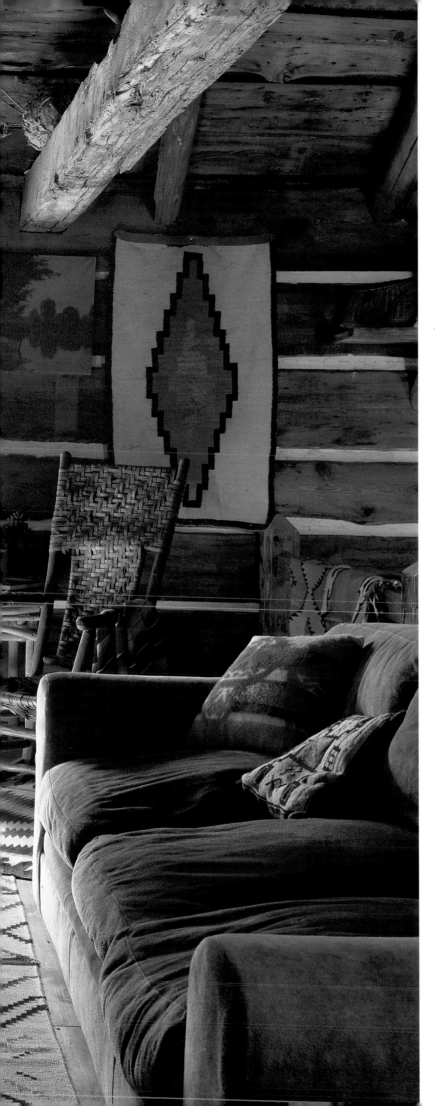

"armoire". These were simple box-like structures, but were, significantly, fitted with a door. Their main use seems to have been for storing food and other goods. Today, cupboards of all types serve a variety of useful functions and feature in the living room, and elsewhere, for many and varied general-storage purposes.

A cupboard in a country-style living room is an ideal candidate for a range of decorative paint treatments, including stencilling, woodgraining, and distressing. In the past, cupboards and many other items of furniture in cottages and country houses were painted with milk paint (see page 146 for details) in a range of earth colours such as cream, buff, grey-green, duck-egg blue, brick red and ox-blood red. Milk paint was widely used by the early settlers in North America, as the ingredients – buttermilk or skimmed milk, pigment and a little lime – were readily available and the results were pleasing and long-lasting. With age, milk paint takes on an attractive, mellow patina. The effect of wear and tear on a newly painted piece can easily be re-created by gently rubbing the paint here and there with sandpaper or steel wool to reveal the wood beneath.

Left & Above - THE LIVING ROOM OF THIS MASSACHUSETTS HOME IS PART OF A PAIR OF RESTORED BARNS. THE FURNITURE HAS BEEN CHOSEN TO COMPLEMENT THE HIGH CEILINGS AND RUGGED BEAMS, AND INCLUDES A STURDY PINE CUPBOARD AND A SIMPLE HANGING CUPBOARD, BOTH PAINTED AND DISTRESSED.

- CANDLE -
BOX

Small boxes of all types were once a common feature in country households. They were used to hold all manner of things, from salt and spices to knives, spoons and, of course, candles, or whatever else needed to be put away safely where it could be readily found. The earliest examples were wall boxes. These were made either to hang from a peg or nail on the wall or designed to sit up against a wall supported on a table or ledge. In their simplest form, these boxes were lidless. Others, however, did have lids and, as the design developed, further elaboration in the form of the inclusion of drawers took place until in some instances the formerly simple box was transformed into a miniature set of drawers. This evolution is analogous to that of the chest as described on page 124.

Collectors have given names to boxes according to their main use, and in addition to those boxes mentioned above, there are, among others, bobbin boxes, for storing lacemaking bobbins, dice and domino boxes, and pipe and tobacco boxes. Country inns once had tobacco boxes, the locked lids of which were opened by pushing a coin through the slot. This allowed the smoker to fill his pipe and pay for it, on trust.

> *The custom is, before you fill,*
> *To put a penny in the till;*
> *When you have filled, without delay,*
> *Close the lid or sixpence pay.*

Some boxes had no specific use, but were merely for keeping important documents, letters, simple personal treasures, or a valuable book safe. These, appropriately, were known as keeping boxes. Quite often, such boxes were intricately decorated by their owners on the outside with paintings or carvings to attest to the value that was placed on them and their contents.

While it may be difficult for us today, with our built-in cupboards and kitchen cabinets, to appreciate fully just how invaluable these boxes were in the past, they still can serve a useful purpose over and above a decorative one. A candle box makes an ideal letter rack or somewhere to keep the household accounts, while other boxes can be modified to suit all types of modern application.

Right - BELOW THE MANTEL SHELF OF THIS LARGE OPEN HEARTH, TO THE LEFT, HANGS A SMALL WALL BOX IN THE SAME DESIGN AS THAT GIVEN IN THE PROJECT THAT FOLLOWS. HERE, IT SERVES AS A USEFUL STORAGE PLACE FOR CANDLES READY FOR USE, OR POSSIBLY FOR TAPERS TO LIGHT THE FIRE.

8in
(203)

9in
(228)

18in
(457)

10in
(254)

5in
(127)

10in
(254)

18in
(457)

10in
(254)

8in
(203)

9in
(228)

8in
(203)

6½in
(165)

ABILITY LEVEL: Novice/Intermediate

SIZE: 18 x 9 x 6½in (457 x 228 x 165mm)

MATERIALS: Pine, Cherry, Oak

CUTTING LIST:
1 back
18 x 8 x ½in (457 x 203 x 12mm)

1 front
8 x 8 x ½in (203 x 203 x 12mm)

2 sides
10 x 5 x ½in (254 x 127 x 12mm)

1 bottom
9 x 6½ x ½in (228 x 165 x 12mm)

See template patterns on page 152 for shaped and cut-out pieces.

All measurements are given in inches, with the equivalents in millimetres indicated in brackets.

2in
(51)

8in
(203)

5in
(127)

6½in
(165)

METHOD:

1. Mark out and cut the separate pieces to size. They can be cut economically from two pieces of wood as shown. Mark each piece for its intended use.

2. Trace the full-sized template patterns on page 152 and transfer the shapes to the appropriate pieces of wood.

3. Cut the pieces to shape.

4. For the internal heart shape, first drill through the wood and then enlarge the hole with a fret saw or coping saw. Finish off with a file and glasspaper.

5. Clean off all tool marks on the sawn edges. Check that everything is cut to size and that the side pieces are a matching pair.

6. Assemble the back, front and side pieces, without using glue. Check the alignment of the matching edges of the shaped pieces. Make any necessary adjustments.

7. Mark out and cut a ¼in (6mm) chamfer on the front and side top edges of the bottom piece of wood.

8. Clean up all the component pieces ready for assembly.

9. Glue and nail all the box components together. Use small panel pins or lost-head nails and take care not to split the wood when nailing, especially if you have used a hardwood to make the box (see page 141 for advice on nailing).

10. Begin by fixing the back to the sides, then add the front. Check that everything is square before fixing the bottom in place. Remove any surplus glue and leave to dry thoroughly.

11. Punch nail heads below the surface and fill the indentations with woodfiller or with a mixture of glue and sawdust.

12. Apply a suitable indoor finish. A traditional beeswax polish will give a warm glow to the wood, especially after a number of applications; varnish will give a tougher, more protective finish. If you want to give your box a well-aged appearance, try one of the special techniques such as distressing the wood, applying an "antique" wood stain, or painting the box and then distressing the paintwork (see pages 146-7 for details).

13. The box can be hung on a wall using two nails, hooks or small pegs through the heart-shaped cut-out, or you can use a standard mirror plate that screws onto the back of the box. The candle box can also be freestanding and be placed on a table or perhaps a window ledge.

Above - A fine collection of kitchen artefacts includes a candle box and a wooden scoop with a decorative chip-carved handle (only partly shown).

Left - This candle box was made by following the instructions given in this project. To complete the look, it was treated with a clear antique finish.

Before the notion of intensive farming became a reality, and the introduction of milking machines a necessity, individual cows in old-style dairies were milked by hand. For centuries, ever since the domestication of the cow, there had been no other way and, indeed, mechanical milking became possible only when an automated mechanism that imitated the quite complex movements of the human hand was perfected.

While milking by hand, the farm lad or dairy maid would sit on a low, sturdy stool, usually constructed with three legs in a tripod arrangement. Even if never used for this specific purpose, such three-legged stools are today collectively known as milking stools. The splayed arrangement of legs was a necessary functional design, for it provided stability on the often uneven stone or dry earth floors that were typical of early farm buildings. And for milking purposes, the tripod of legs served another important need – they allowed the sitter to lean forward on two legs, "into" the cow, without losing balance.

The majority of milking stools have circular seats or tops, although some have a straight front edge with a pair of legs at each corner and a round back edge with a central third leg. This design, too, can be easily tilted forward. Stools with square seats and four legs are more likely to have been for domestic use. A Scandinavian speciality has only one leg. Early designs had riven (cleft) legs, split from a log and roughly shaped by drawknifing, or were made from suitable branchwood. Legs were commonly joined to the tops by means of through joints secured not by glue but by wedging. It is possible that, in the absence of a boring tool, leg holes would have been burned through the seat with a red-hot iron bar.

Even if you don't keep a domestic cow about the house, as was very commonplace in country regions throughout Europe and North America until relatively recent times, a milking stool will still make a positive contribution to a living room fireside or a country-style kitchen. Children also love them because they don't stand too high off the ground. But a word of caution is needed here: don't allow anybody to stand on them because with only three legs they can easily topple over if the weight is off-centre.

Left - A LATE 18TH-CENTURY COUNTRY HOUSE IN VAKSALA, SWEDEN, PROVIDES THE IDEAL SETTING FOR A RANGE OF AUTHENTIC SWEDISH RUSTIC FURNITURE. IN FRONT OF THE BLAZING FIRE SITS A 19TH-CENTURY PINE MILKING STOOL, WELL WORN FROM YEARS OF SERVICE.

ABILITY LEVEL: Novice/Intermediate

SIZE: 10 x 10 x 8in (254 x 254 x 203mm)

MATERIALS:
(**Top**) Elm, Oak, Pine
(**Legs**) Ash, Beech, Maple, Oak

CUTTING LIST:
1 top
10 x 10 x 2in (254 x 254 x 51mm)

3 legs
8 x 2 x 2in (203 x 51 x 51mm)

All measurements are given in inches, with the equivalents in millimetres indicated in brackets.

METHOD:

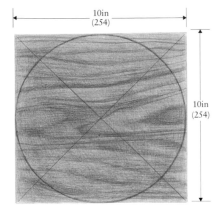

1. Using a pair of compasses, mark out the top piece to a 10in (254mm) diameter circle and cut to shape.

2. Choose the best surface to be the top and, with the compasses still set to give a 5in (127mm) radius, mark off six equal points around the circumference of the top piece.

3. Join these six points with pencil lines and on these mark the three leg positions for drilling 1¾in (44mm) in from the edge.

4. These three holes are drilled at a compound angle of 20° from the vertical. This can be done by eye, but only if you are very

experienced. There are various techniques to help you to get this angle right. A simple way is to use a carpenter's sliding bevel set at 20° as a guide when drilling.

5. However, a more accurate method of working is to construct a pre-drilled guide block as shown here. When correctly made and cramped to the work, all you need to do is drill into the stool seat through the hole in the guide block.

6. Where a pillar drill is available, it is best to tilt the stool top and drill vertically into it. To do this, tilt the stool top up at the prescribed angle by raising one end on a block. Another, more secure, method is to make a tilting-table arrangement, as shown. Use a protractor to measure the angle of the table top, which is fixed by means of a supporting block. By aligning each pencil line on the stool top with a centre reference line drawn on the tilting table, consistently angled holes for the stool legs are assured.

7. Drill three 1in (25mm) diameter holes through the top. A saw-toothed bit is recommended (see page 139 for advice on drills).

8. Clean up the sawn edges of the top and bevel the edges for comfort.

9. Now turn your attention to the stool legs. These can be turned on a lathe, if one is available, using the dimensions given. However, stool legs were frequently shaped using a drawknife or spokeshave either to a roughly round section or an approximately hexagonal shape. A plane could also be used.

2in (51)
8in (203)

10. No matter which technique is used, the legs must be tapered at the top to carefully made round tenon joints 1in (25mm) diameter and about 2in (51mm) in length. This is best done with a spokeshave, but a rasp or file can be used.

11. Form each joint individually and try it frequently for size in the appropriate socket in the stool top. Bear in mind that although

the joint should be a good fit it does not have to be too tight at this stage, since it will be secured later by wedges.

12. When all three legs fit, mark pencil lines on their ends to indicate the orientation of the saw cuts needed for the wedges. It is important that the wedges are inserted at right-angles to the grain of the wood of the stool top. Otherwise the force of the wedge could easily split the wood.

13. Remove the legs and make 1¼in(32mm) saw cuts for the wedges.

¼in (6)

1½in (38)

14. Following the dimensions given, make three wedges. Always use a hardwood for the wedges. Make sure that the grain runs down the length of the wedge and not across its width. Try using wood of a contrasting colour to give the wedges an added decorative touch.

15. Clean up all the component pieces. Prepare to assemble the stool by first inserting a little glue into each leg socket. Next, fit the legs so that their tops protrude slightly through the top of the stool.

16. Align each leg so that the wedges will lie at right-angles to the grain of the seat (see step 12 above).

17. Stand the stool upright on a flat, solid surface. Fit the wedges and tap each one part way in using a hammer. Then tap each one

again in turn until they are tightly fitting. The weight of a hammer is better for this than a wooden mallet.

18. Check the stability of the stool, wipe off any surplus glue and leave it to dry.

19. When it is dry, saw off the protruding stub ends of the legs and wedges almost flush with the stool seat, taking care not to damage its surface. Clean off the saw marks with a sharp chisel or block plane.

20. Mark and then saw or rasp off the inside bottom edges of each leg close to the angle made with the floor surface.

21. Smooth the completed stool with a fine-grade abrasive paper, if necessary.

22. Apply a suitable finish (see pages 146-7 for advice). Traditionally, milking stools were left unfinished. Those used in the dairy were scrubbed clean using coarse sand.

DUCK
DECOY

More than a thousand years ago, native Americans used dead and artificial birds as decoys to lure wild duck and other fowl within range of their weapons. These early artificial decoys were in the main quite crudely made, comprising bundles of aquatic rush either covered in real duck skins or simply painted and decorated with feathers. Other examples of decoys were nothing more than piles of mud and clay and bunches of dried grass tied on to sticks.

In Europe, a different method of wildfowling predominated. There, semi-domesticated living birds were used to entice their unsuspecting brethren into specially made, tunnel-shaped capture nets. These lures were known as Coy Ducks, a name derived from the Dutch word *Ende-Kooy*, meaning a duck cage or trap and the original application of the word decoy.

When the first European settlers arrived in America, they found it expedient to adopt the local method as there were no domestic animals or birds readily to hand and "living off the land" became a stark reality. In due course, however, dissatisfaction with the temporary and largely land-bound Indian decoy led to the introduction of a more permanent, floating decoy made from wood. Very simply constructed at first, and often blackened by charring in a fire or crudely painted, these early wooden decoys were more representational than realistic. Properly ballasted and anchored

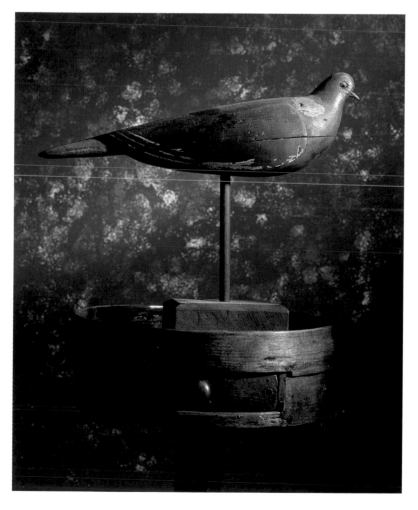

by stone weights, however, they bobbed about in quite a lifelike manner, and even the crudest were generally successful in attracting unwitting live birds. Later decoys became more sophisticated in construction and finish, and those from individual makers were extolled for their realism and their claimed effectiveness as lures.

The decoy method relies on the "instinct to forgather" of many species of wild water fowl, and other birds too. For many, this trait resulted in extinction, or near extinction, as literally tens of thousands of birds fell each year, particularly during annual migratory flights, largely to "market gunners". These professional and expert marksmen shot in order to supply both a commercial market and an ever-increasing population. Such activity required a large number of decoys – a typical lone gunner might shoot over a "rig" of 40 to 50 decoys and bag hundreds of birds in a day. For a period, demand could be satisfied only by resorting to factory-made decoys, but these were never as attractive or as well made and decorated as the hand-made decoys.

Today, the law forbids duck shooting on this scale, although sport shooting is still permitted in season and under licence. And decoys are still made and used along the shoreline and in the marshes, but many, particularly old ones, are now used only decoratively, and the very best of these have become highly desirable and extremely collectable.

Left - A PARTICULARLY FINE COLLECTION OF LOCALLY MADE DECOYS BRIGHTENS UP THE MATT, EARTHY COLOURS OF THIS NORTH AMERICAN COLONIAL HOME. THE ARM CHAIR, WHICH PROBABLY DATES FROM THE 17TH CENTURY, IS A NINE-SPINDLE DOUBLE-COMB BACK, A RARE NORTH AMERICAN WINDSOR VARIANT.

Above - DECOYS ARE MOST OFTEN OF THE FLOATING TYPE, BUT THE FORERUNNERS OF THESE, THE PROTOTYPE NORTH AMERICAN INDIAN DECOYS, WERE MADE PRIMARILY FOR USE ON LAND. LAND-BOUND DECOYS WERE KNOWN AS "STICK-UPS", OF WHICH THE ABOVE IS A TYPICAL EXAMPLE.

ABILITY LEVEL: Intermediate

SIZE: 11 x 6 x 5in (279 x 152 x 127mm)

MATERIALS: Pine

CUTTING LIST:
Body: 1 piece
11 x 5 x 3in (279 x 127 x 76mm)

or Body: 2 pieces
11 x 2½ x 3in (279 x 63 x 76mm)

Head
5½ x 2½ x 1½in (140 x 63 x 38mm)

1 dowel
2 x ½in (51 x 12mm) diameter

See template patterns on page 150 for the head and body.

All measurements are given in inches, with the equivalents in millimetres indicated in brackets.

METHOD:

1. In making solid bodies, the early decoy maker would first cut the wood to length and then proceed to chop the block into the rough shape required using a sharp axe. Working at a chopping block of convenient height, he would first remove the corners, roughly round the breast, and shape the tail.

2. Next, with the roughly shaped body held in a vice, a drawknife or spokeshave was used to refine the shape. An area at the forward end was kept slightly oversize and flat to receive the head. In this process the maker used no patterns or templates, relying only on his skill and experience to achieve the required shape.

3. The head, which demands more careful attention, was sawn to profile, according to the species of bird, and then, with the wood held in a vice, it was bored to receive a fixing dowel or nail.

4. The shape of the assembled decoy was then finished off using a spokeshave or by whittling with a knife and finally sanded smooth before being painted.

5. To make a modern decoy, particularly one intended as an ornament, use the dimensions given and cut the body to size. If you are using two pieces of wood for the body, first glue them together and allow the glue to dry thoroughly before proceeding.

6. Using the template patterns given on page 150, begin the preliminary shaping using a saw. If you feel you have the necessary skill, an axe can be used for this.

7. Once you have the basic outline shape, start the detailed shaping using a drawknife or spokeshave, woodcarving tools, or knife. Reference to the cross-sections given in the templates will prove helpful in achieving the required shape (see page 150). For safety, work with the wood in a vice or cramped to the bench during the shaping process.

8. Finish off the shaping with a file or knife, remembering to keep the forward area oversize and flat at this stage to accommodate the head.

9. Using the template on page 150, cut the head to shape using a bandsaw or coping saw. Make sure its base is square and flat.

10. Using a blind dowel is the best method of fixing the head to the body of a decorative decoy. For this, drill a ½in (12mm) hole down through the head and fit and glue a piece of dowel in place. In addition to fixing the head, this dowel also provides a convenient grip for holding the wood while you finish the final shaping.

11. Grip the base of the head piece in the vice and shape the main part of the head (using the template pattern and drawn details as a guide). Finish off the detailing and the area around the base of the head, with the dowel already in place held in the vice. Take care not to crush the dowel.

½in (12)
diameter

12. Mark and drill the dowel hole in the body. Lightly plane the flat area left on the body to make a level jointing surface. Try the head for fit, without using glue, and adjust the mating surfaces if necessary until they fit comfortably. Then glue the head to the body and leave it to dry.

13. You can now finish off any of the detailing of the decoy, filing and finally smoothing the surface ready for painting.

14. The paint finishes on early decoys were usually quite dull earth colours, and very little detailing, such as feathers or even eyes, was included. You can emulate this style and keep everything simple or try to produce a more realistic appearance. The body shape and head of this decoy approximate to that of a male mallard and it may be finished in an appropriate plumage and colours. For reference, you could use a colour photograph as a painting guide. See also pages 146-7 for advice on painting.

Below - AGAINST THE LIGHT-WASHED BACKGROUND OF A PINE-BOARDED WALL, A DUCK DECOY SITTING IN AN UNUSED SEED TRAY MAKES A PLEASING, THREE-DIMENSIONAL STILL-LIFE PICTURE. A SEASONED PINE BENCH SITS COMFORTABLY BELOW IT.

CANDLE STAND

There is evidence that candle making was established as a trade in Europe as early as the 13th century. At first, candles would have been made with tallow – basically animal fat, which gives off a terrible stench when burned – but beeswax would also have been used. Although more expensive than tallow, beeswax has a far more agreeable aroma. However, it was the use of paraffin wax, first made in America by Abraham Gesner in 1846 and developed commercially by the Scotsman James Young, that made candles less objectionable and more affordable, and ensured their popular and widespread use, even to the present day. Whenever soft lights and a romantic setting are called for, candles suit the occasion.

Candles are most often used in some form of candle holder, often a candlestick with a socket just large enough to accommodate the base of the candle. This would have been placed where the candle's limited throw of light could be used to best advantage. When extra height was needed, the candle stand was once a popular choice.

Candle stands are related to that group of furniture that includes pedestal and tripod tables; similarities in their design and construction are fairly obvious, and they differ mainly in terms of size and sophistication. An early reference is contained in an 11th-century manuscript now in the British Museum, which describes a small, round table on a central pillar above spreading feet. Candle stands probably reached their zenith of popularity in England shortly after the Restoration of Charles II in the 17th century, when highly ornate examples, along with equally ornate wall mirrors, became fashionable in the extravagant drawing rooms of the period.

The candle stand that features here, however, is entirely utilitarian. It is simply made and solidly constructed, and is typical of the type used every day in Europe and in the early colonial period in North America. While some designs, including those of the Shakers, often incorporate a tripod arrangement of "feet" dovetailed into a lathe-turned column, this one features a more easily made, and stronger, cross-lapped-base construction. The square stem, which is chamfered into an octagonal shape, is secured to the base using a substantial dowel or mortise and tenon joints.

Right - THE CANDLE STAND CAN FULFIL A WIDE RANGE OF FUNCTIONS IN THE MODERN HOME. HERE IT IS A HANDY DEPOSITORY FOR BOOKS, BUT IT COULD EQUALLY WELL SERVE AS A PEDESTAL FOR A FRESH OR DRIED FLOWER ARRANGEMENT, OR AS A STAND FOR A PIECE OF SCULPTURE.

ABILITY LEVEL: Intermediate

SIZE: 27 x 13 x 13in (686 x 330 x 330mm)

MATERIALS: Cherry, Oak

CUTTING LIST:
1 stem
24 x 2¼ x 2¼in (610 x 57 x 57mm)

1 top
12 x 12 x 1in (305 x 305 x 25mm)

1 brace
10 x 2 x 1in (254 x 51 x 25mm)

2 feet
13½ x 2½ x 2in (343 x 63 x 51mm)

1 dowel
3 x 1in (76 x 25mm) diameter

All measurements are given in inches, with the equivalents in millimetres indicated in brackets.

METHOD:

1. If you cannot obtain the top as one piece of wood, you will have to edge join narrower pieces together (see page 141 for advice).

2. Make sure that the top is flat. If you have glued pieces together, wait until the glue is dry, and then plane the surfaces clean and smooth while the wood is still square (it is easier to hold at this stage).

3. Next, cut the top to a 12in (305mm) diameter circle. Clean up the sawn edges and round over or chamfer them slightly, top and bottom.

4. Cut the stem to length, making sure that both ends are square. Mark out the chamfers in pencil as a guide to planing. The finger gauging method on page 137 is accurate enough for this task.

5. Plane the four chamfers to produce the required octagonal shape. Allow the chamfers to taper off, leaving the top 4in(102mm) square for the top lapped, or bridle, joint.

6. Make the bottom joint by drilling into the bottom of the stem and gluing in a piece of 1in (25mm) diameter dowel. This peg joint will fit into a corresponding hole drilled into the assembled feet (see step 12 on the page opposite). Drilled holes must be perfectly perpendicular to the stem.

7. As an alternative, this round joint can be worked in the solid on the end of the stem. Or a conventional, square, mortise and tenon could be used instead (see page 144). In each case, add an extra 1½in (38mm) to the stem length given.

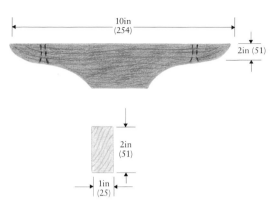

13. The brace that supports the top is lapped, full width, into the top of the stem, making what is also known as a bridle joint. Shape and then fit the brace to the underside of the top, as shown. It should lie across the grain of the top piece. Glue and screw it into position.

14. Mark out and carefully cut the housing for the brace on the top of the stem. Take your measurements from the brace itself since they may differ from those given. Check the joint for a good fit; it should not be too tight, since forcing it may split the stem.

8. Now start making the feet. The two pieces are cross lapped or half lapped so that the top is flush where they cross over.

9. Mark out and cut each half of the joint as shown (see also page 143 for guidance). Check for a good, tight fit, make any adjustments that are necessary, and then take the joint apart.

10. Mark out and cut the scrolled shape of the two feet. Sand back the sawn surfaces and chamfer the top edges.

11. Reassemble the feet to make sure they fit and then glue the joint and cramp/clamp the wood together if necessary. Wipe off surplus glue and leave it to dry.

12. When dry, if using the dowel method, drill a 1in (25mm) hole through the centre of the cross lap. If a mortise and tenon is used, mark out and cut the mortise square through the centre of the cross lap joint. Check this joint for a good, tight fit with the stem dowel. Separate the pieces for the next stage.

15. Disassemble and clean up all the surfaces. When satisfied, glue the stem into the base feet. For extra security, the joint can be wedged (see page 29 for advice).

16. Next, glue the top into place by fitting the brace into its prepared housing. Secure

this by drilling two holes through the assembled joint and inserting ¼in (6mm) dowel pegs, as shown. When the glue is dry, either cut these off flush or leave them slightly proud of the surface.

17. Remove any surplus glue and clean up all the surfaces.

18. In the past, the candle stand would either have been stained and polished or left its natural colour and given a protective finish using beeswax. A wax finish will bring out the warm colours of the wood, and over time, and many applications, the colour will become richer and deeper. You can achieve this effect more quickly by applying wood stain, and then a coat of wax or perhaps a clear varnish (see pages 146-7 for advice on techniques for finishing).

SIDE TABLE

Tables in medieval times were only temporary affairs – nothing more than a long board, or series of boards butted up together to make a wider surface, supported on wooden trestles. When the meal was finished, these trestle tables could easily be dismantled and removed. This type of furniture suited an era when communal living was commonplace and rooms were not specifically designated as having different functions as they are today. An interesting historical note is that "board" in this context is still used in such terms as "boarding house" and "board and lodgings". Over the years, board and trestle were joined together into a more permanent piece of furniture, which became known as the standing or "dormant" table. Chaucer, writing in the 14th century, refers to "his table dormant in his halle always". However, sometime early in the 16th century table design changed significantly with the introduction of the frame construction, which gave rise to the "joyned" table.

Instead of a pair of trestles, the table now had four (or more) legs linked and braced by right-angled cross-rails at the top and stretcher rails at the bottom. All of this arrangement was mortised and tenoned together and carefully pegged for extra strength and stability. Many of these tables were of considerable size. But as domestic arrangements and architecture changed, so a need arose for different

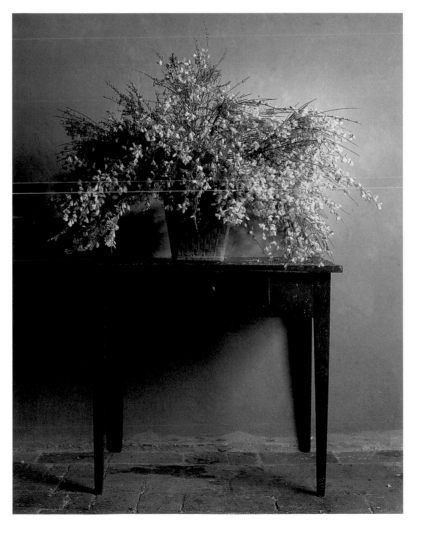

kinds of furniture, including smaller-sized tables. Initially, these were cut-down versions of the larger tables. Later they became lighter in construction and soon began to diversify markedly in style and construction, including all kinds of clever contrivances to make smaller tables extendable into larger ones.

Today there is a style of table suitable for virtually every room in the house and for all manner of specific occasions and uses. One frequently seen design is the side table, which was first developed in the early 17th century. The side table usually has a square or rectangular top; in earlier times, pairs were often made to stand at each end of a formal dining area. Some side tables also come with a semicircular top.

The small side table shown here serves a number of potential functions. Its name gives it its proper position – it should be placed to one side against a wall where it might function as a writing table or as a small work table. Its large drawer is useful in both these roles. It would be equally at home in a kitchen. In the past, tables of this kind were generally made of a hardwood frame for strength with an inexpensive top constructed out of softwood, such as pine. Everything would be stained to match. However, if the table was destined for the kitchen, the top would not be stained so that it could be kept clean by a scouring with water and gritty sand.

Left - A SIMPLY MADE SIDE TABLE SUCH AS THIS GIVES A REAL FLAVOUR OF COUNTRY LIVING. IN MANY CASES, THE UNDERFRAME WOULD BE MADE FROM SOME TYPE OF HARDWOOD, TO GIVE STRENGTH TO THE CONSTRUCTION, WHILE THE TOP WOULD BE OF PINE FOR ECONOMY.

Above - RESPLENDENT WITH A CASUAL ARRANGEMENT OF FLOWERING WILD BROOM, THIS SIDE TABLE HAS AN OAK UNDERFRAME AND A TOP OF YELLOW PINE. A USEFUL DRAWER IS INCLUDED IN ITS CONSTRUCTION, WHICH IS DESCRIBED IN DETAIL IN THE PROJECT THAT FOLLOWS.

ABILITY LEVEL: Experienced

SIZE: 36 x 30 x 22in (914 x 762 x 559mm)

MATERIALS:
(**Top**) Pine
(**Frame**) Oak, Cherry, Beech

CUTTING LIST:
1 top
36 x 22 x ⅞in (914 x 559 x 22mm)

4 legs
28 x 2½ x 2½in (711 x 63 x 63mm)

2 side rails
27½ x 5 x ⅞in (699 x 127 x 22mm)

2 end rails
13½ x 5 x ⅞in (343 x 127 x 22mm)

2 cross rails
14 x 2 x ⅞in (356 x 51 x 22mm)

2 drawer runners
13 x ⅞ x ⅞in (330 x 22 x 22mm)

1 drawer front
16 x 3½ x ⅞in (406 x 89 x 22mm)

2 drawer sides
12 x 3½ x ½in (305 x 89 x 12mm)

1 drawer back
16 x 3 x ½in (406 x 76 x 12mm)

1 drawer bottom
13 x 16 x ¼in (330 x 406 x 6mm)

All measurements are given in inches, with the equivalents in millimetres indicated in brackets.

METHOD:

1. The top is made by edge joining narrower boards. Begin by selecting straight pieces of pine, planing their mating edges and joining them using the simple "rubbed joint", or an alternative method described on pages 141-2. If the top is to be left untreated for kitchen use, apply a waterproof glue.

2. Glue up the top. Check that it is flat, apply glue to the mating edges and use a minimum of three cramps as shown and described on page 142.

3. Cut the frame materials to size. The legs are tapered and the frame is fixed together with double mortise and tenon joints (see pages 144-5 for advice on this joint).

4. Mark the top ends of the legs with a pencil line as shown as a useful guide for all subsequent work.

5. Taper the legs on two inside surfaces only, leaving the top 6in (152mm) of the legs untapered. Remove the bulk of the waste wood by sawing followed by hand planing. Sand the edges to remove the sharp edges.

6. Mark out the double mortise positions on the legs. Cut the mortises, keeping them straight and square. Note the recesses for the tenon haunch and central tongue.

7. Mark out the double tenons as shown on the side and end rails. Cut the tenons

straight and square. Remember the haunch and central tongue (see page 145).

8. Test fit the tenons into their respective mortises. Trim as required for a good fit.

9. Assemble the legs and the side and end rails, without using glue, and check that everything fits well and is square.

10. Check the position of the cut-out for the drawer and the position and required length (including the stub tenons) of the two internal cross rails, which support and strengthen the frame. Disassemble.

11. Mark out and cut the drawer opening on the front side rail. This opening should finish at 16in x 3½in (406 x 89mm).

12. Mark the position of the mortises for the cross rails on the inside surfaces of the side rails. Ensure that the cross rails will be parallel. Cut the mortises carefully, no more than ½in (12mm) deep.

13. Mark out the stub tenons on the cross rails. Cut these and check them individually for a good fit. The cross rails should be just flush with the drawer opening.

14. Trial assemble the complete frame, including the cross rails, which must be put in position first. Disassemble.

15. If the leg joints are to be additionally secured with wooden pins, these should be prepared now (see page 145 for "draw boring"). Clean off all surface marks and prepare for gluing.

16. Glue and assemble the complete frame. Fit the cross rails first, then join the rails to the legs. Hold them with cramps or insert securing pegs. Check that the frame is square, clean off surplus glue and leave until the glue has completely dried.

17. Prepare and fit the drawer runners. Screw these into place rather than gluing them. They should be just flush with the drawer opening and parallel to each other.

3½in (89)

2⅞in (73)

¼in (6)

¼in (6)

⅞in (22)

18. Make the drawer. It has lapped dovetails at the front, through dovetails at the back (see page 143). Plane the drawer front to a good, tight fit in the drawer opening. Cut the drawer back to the same length, or slightly under, and the side pieces to the same width as the front. Check that the ends are square and mark adjoining pieces.

19. Cut the groove for the drawer bottom in the front piece and both side pieces. (See diagram at top of page.)

20. Mark out and cut the dovetail joints, the "tails" first, on each end of the side pieces. Use the measurements and proportions given above and see page 143 for method.

21. Mark out the dovetail "sockets" using the "tails" cut in step 20 as a template. Cut them out (see page 143 for method).

22. Test fit each joint, as little as possible, and adjust as necessary for a good fit. Assemble the drawer, without glue, and check for square. Disassemble and clean off any surface marks.

23. Apply glue and assemble the drawer. Cramp it together, check that it is square, and leave it to dry.

24. Measure the required size for the drawer bottom. The grain should run from side to side. Trim it to fit the groove at the front and sides (it passes underneath the back). The bottom is not glued, but is held in place by screwing or pinning where it passes under the drawer back.

25. When the drawer is dry, clean off in the joint areas. Try it for fit in the drawer opening. Adjust for a good sliding fit.

26. Fit the drawer stops as shown – it is easier to do this before fitting the top.

2in (51)

1in (25)

2in (51)

¾in (19)

27. Make or buy a knob for the drawer. Drill a tight hole for the shaft and glue it into place. Secure it with a wedge if possible.

28. You can now fit the top. Using "buttons" is the usual method of doing this. These screw to the top, but are held in grooves in the side rails and are free to slide in order to

allow for any movement of the wood. The step of the button should be slightly less than the distance between the groove and the rail edge in order to keep the top pulled downward. Make sure the screws are not too long. Fit two buttons at each end and two along each side.

29. Before fitting the top, plane the top surface to a good finish. Plane its edges smooth and bevel over the top edges and corners. Then fit as described in step 28.

30. The frame may be stained darker or left as it is and given a finish appropriate for its use (see pages 146-7). The pine top may also be given a clear finish; if it is to go in the kitchen, the top may be left untreated and kept clean by scrubbing.

Right - THIS SMALL TABLE, WITH ITS ELEGANT TAPERED LEGS AND USEFUL DRAWER, IS SIMILAR IN CONSTRUCTION TO THE SIDE TABLE. HERE, IT IS USED TO SUPPORT A MODERN READING LAMP, BUT ITS TIMELESS SIMPLICITY IS IN KEEPING WITH THE WOODEN PANELLING ON THE WALL AND THE COLONIAL CARVER CHAIR.

Wood Outside

A liking for the country life implies a love of the outdoors, for the two concepts are inseparable. Naturalness and a lack of pretention are at the very heart of the notion of country style, and how better to feel close to nature – even if only at weekends when you can get a few days away from the concrete of the city streets – than being outside with the sun on your back and the good earth under your feet? And what better than the naturalness of wood to celebrate this affinity?

WOOD AS A BUILDING MATERIAL

Wood as a building material has a long association with mankind, from the simple, often temporary shelters of our early ancestors to the solidly permanent, timber-framed buildings of medieval times; from the rough-hewn log cabins common in the high-forest regions of Europe, and used again and again by colonial pioneers everywhere, to the weatherboarded, shingle-roofed houses typical of the east coast of North America. The early settlers built their homes using the material they found most readily to hand – and where there happened to be an abundance of trees, wood, of course, predominated. The manner in which they built, however, was strongly influenced by the traditions of their native homelands and also, to some extent, by the type and size of the local trees and the size and durability of the logs they yielded.

TRANSITIONARY SPACE

Many of these ethnic building styles had one notable architectural feature in common, however – the porch, or verandah. In fact, "verandah" is a Hindi word, as is bungalow, which was absorbed into the language in the days of the British Raj in India. Built as a type of covered, but usually open-sided, extension to a house, the porch is where the inside meets the outside, and where the distinction between the two often becomes blurred.

Its construction and character can vary enormously, from the formal to the strictly functional, from the rustic to the ramshackle. Where a porch is not regularly maintained by painting, its timbers soon begin to weather, taking on the colours of the countryside and strengthening the ever-present link with nature.

Depending on its geographical location or the season of the year, the porch may function as a much-used outdoor room, or have only limited, more occasional use. Where the climate is mild or there are long, hot summers, the porch provides essential shade and, being in regular use, will probably have its own permanent furniture and fittings – like any other room of the house. Where the climate is less temperate, however, and the weather more uncertain, the porch will be more irregularly used and will need furnishings that can be easily carried indoors and out.

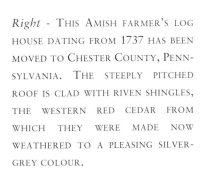

Right - THIS AMISH FARMER'S LOG HOUSE DATING FROM 1737 HAS BEEN MOVED TO CHESTER COUNTY, PENN-SYLVANIA. THE STEEPLY PITCHED ROOF IS CLAD WITH RIVEN SHINGLES, THE WESTERN RED CEDAR FROM WHICH THEY WERE MADE NOW WEATHERED TO A PLEASING SILVER-GREY COLOUR.

Far right - RUSTIC FURNITURE, TYPI-CAL OF THAT ASSOCIATED WITH THE ADIRONDACK REGION OF NORTHERN NEW YORK STATE, FILLS THIS PORCH. THAT, AND THE SUPPORTING CORNER POSTS OF THE BARE, WEATHERED TREE TRUNKS, BRINGS A FEELING OF THE FOREST CLOSER TO THE LIVING SPACE.

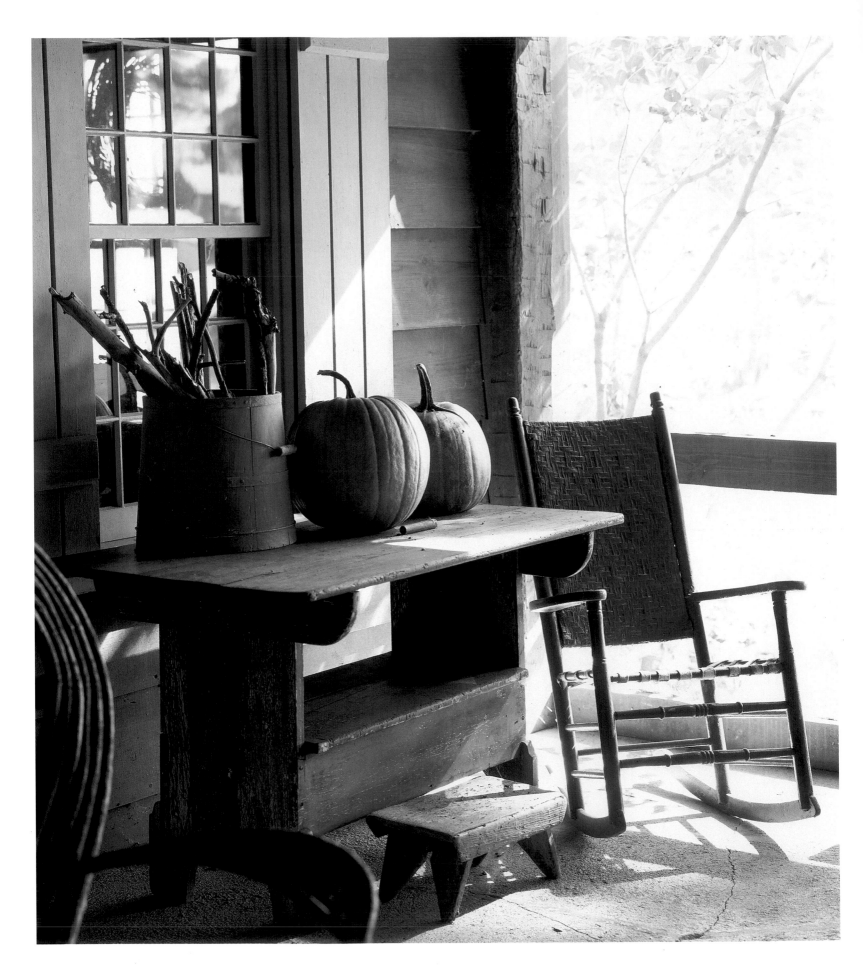

WOODEN FURNITURE

A small table or bench has many uses outdoors and, in particular, the simple five-board bench suits a verandah or porch extremely well. It is easily made by assembling the prepared components, without requiring too many carpentry skills, and it was among the earliest pieces made by country woodworkers in many different countries. Its method of construction makes it a very adaptable piece of furniture. It can be built in a variety of useful sizes, from foot stools to tables, and its inherent simplicity ranks it along with the best of traditional country style.

In most people's minds, the quintessential piece of porch furniture must be the rocking chair. A late 18th-century innovation, the rocking chair was at first known by the name "digestive chair", an affirmation of its perceived use then and now. The admission by some unknown early devotee of the rocker that ". . . sometimes I rocks and thinks and sometimes I just rocks" encapsulates the totally relaxing image of the old rocking chair out on the back porch.

Chairs that rock, and others that don't, are made in all shapes and sizes, and many styles are suitable for porch or garden use. It is a historical fact that Windsor chairs were originally much used outside in English gardens, many painted green for that specific purpose. And it appears that similar chairs were used in some London parks and cricket grounds up until about the turn of the 19th century. Another style of chair, the lath or ladderback Shaker-style chair with woven seat, is eminently suitable for outdoor use and is frequently used in this way. The austere yet graceful shapes of these chairs, either rockers or stationary, are entirely in keeping with the simplicity of country life.

Chairs, benches, and other items of furniture made in what is generally known as the rustic style, are also extremely popular as both porch and garden furniture, as well as in some situations indoors. Rustic style combines country living with natural history: part furniture, part tree, it is a synthesis of man and nature, a union of the maker's mind and the spirits of the forest.

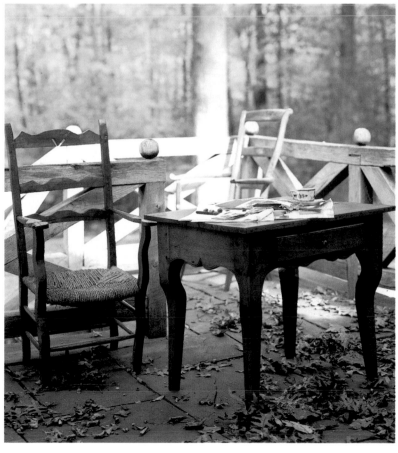

Left - THIS TABLE CONVERTS TO A HIGH-BACK SEAT; IT IS A NEW ENGLAND VERSION OF THE SO-CALLED MONK'S BENCH.

Above Right - WHAT COULD BE MORE INVITING THAN A ROCKING CHAIR SITTING ON A SHELTERED PORCH, THE VERY EPITOME OF EASE AND RELAXATION?

Below Right - A SMALL LADDERBACK CHAIR AND SIDE TABLE – STRAGGLERS FROM SUMMER – WAIT TO BE TAKEN INDOORS AS THE NEW ENGLAND FALL BEGINS.

BIRD
HOUSE

One of the additional pleasures of having a town garden, or of living in a more rural setting, is the relationship you can build up with the resident animals of the not-too-wild variety – especially small birds. If given regular inducements of food, birds will readily adopt your garden as part of their feeding territory, even becoming quite regular in their visits to collect your daily offerings. Attracting birds into the garden – an urban one, one set among forests or farmland, or even to the window ledge of a city apartment – depends on more than just food, however. Equally important are the other necessities of life, such as water and shelter.

Feeding the birds can range from occasionally throwing out scraps of left-over food to keeping a specially installed bird table or other feeding devices regularly stocked. Catering for the birds' need for water is usually by means of a bird bath, elaborate and decorative, or simple and utilitarian. The design really does not matter to the birds – as long as it is not too restricted in width or too deep for the likely bathers – and should be of a style that matches the rest of the garden.

Supplying shelter – a simple place for roosting or nesting – is usually achieved by the provision of a nest box. Different species of bird have very different nesting requirements, and a little research will help guarantee that the nesting box you build and install will meet the needs of the birds you wish to attract. The boxes illustrated here, which form the inspiration

for this particular project, are intended to be used by hole-nesting birds such as blue tits, robins and sparrows. But the size of the entrance hole is a critical deciding factor, since invasion by other species of birds, as well as mammalian and reptilian egg stealers, is not uncommon if the recommended dimension is exceeded.

Nest boxes for use outdoors do not have to be finished to a particularly high degree, and certainly not as artistically as the ones pictured. The birds will not mind if the construction lacks some sophistication and finesse, and an exterior that blends with the natural surroundings would probably be more to their liking, too. This project is an excellent starting point for the novice woodworker, since the birds will not be a critical audience. Simply use the correct materials and follow the stage-by-stage construction details carefully

– and don't forget to get the dimensions of the entrance hole right for the birds you want to see using your box.

Of course, bird houses are not limited to being used outside. They also have obvious aesthetic appeal, and this has been seized upon as an interesting interior design idea. They have become increasingly popular as decorative objects in the home, sometimes left in their natural state to bring something of the indoors into a room or on to a porch, but more often painted in matt earth colours as can be seen here. If you intend to encourage nesting birds, however, boxes must be put out by the New Year at the latest.

Above - THIS ATTRACTIVE BIRD HOUSE IS SUIT-ABLE FOR HOLE-NESTING BIRDS.

ABILITY LEVEL: Novice

SIZE: 10 x 8 x 6in (254 x 203 x 152mm)

MATERIALS: Pine
Piece of leather or sheet rubber

CUTTING LIST:
1 front
10 x 6 x ⅝in (254 x 152 x 16mm)

1 back
10 x 6 x ⅝in (254 x 152 x 16mm)

2 sides
7 x 5 x ⅝in (178 x 127 x 16mm)

1 roof side
7½ x 6 x ⅝in (190 x 152 x 16mm)

1 roof side
7 x 6 x ⅝in (178 x 152 x 16mm)

1 floor
8 x 5 x ⅝in (203 x 127 x 16mm)

Note: All pieces can be cut from a single length, 50 x 6 x ⅝in (1270 x 152 x 16mm). A piece of floorboard would be suitable.

All measurements are given in inches, with the equivalents in millimetres indicated in brackets.

METHOD:

1. Begin by marking out the required pieces and saw to size. Mark each piece for its intended use so that there is no confusion later on.

2. Mark out the roof line on the front piece and cut away the waste wood to make the required 45° slope. Mark the position of the entrance hole on the front piece and drill it to the recommended diameter, which is 1⅛in (29mm) for small birds such as tits and robins and 1¼in (32mm) for larger birds such as sparrows. If you don't have a drill of the right size, drill a series of small holes and enlarge them with a file. Smooth the edges of the finished hole.

Slotted hole for hanging

3. Mark out the roof line on the back piece and cut away the waste wood to make the required 45° slope. Make a slotted hole in the back piece for hanging the finished box from a screw or nail.

4. Drill a couple of drainage holes in the floor piece of the box; about ¼in (6mm) in diameter is adequate.

5. Mark out and cut a 45° chamfer on the top edge of each side piece to follow the roof line.

6. Assemble the front, back and side pieces, without glue, and check that the side chamfers align correctly. Adjust as necessary.

7. Glue and nail the front, back and side pieces together. Use a waterproof (outdoor)

glue. Take care when nailing not to split the wood (see page 141 for advice on nailing).

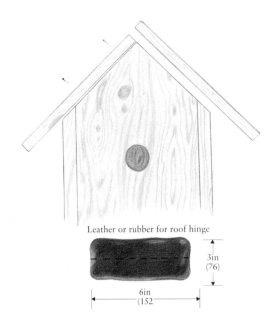

Leather or rubber for roof hinge

3in (76)

6in (152)

8. Put the floor piece into position. Note that there is an overhang to the front and sides. Glue and nail the floor into place, making sure that the structure remains square. Remove surplus glue and leave to dry.

9. Check the roof pieces for fit. Note how the longer piece overlaps the shorter. If all is well, glue and nail them into place.

10. Cover the roof joint with a strip of leather or sheet rubber. Attach this securely with large-headed nails or tacks.

11. If you want to be able to open the box for out-of-season cleaning, only fix the shorter

half of the roof permanently into position. Leave the other loose. with the leather or rub-

Roof catch

12. Secure the hinged half of the roof with a simple catch. The detail illustration shows how to make this from two small fencing staples and a short piece of wire. Take care not to split the wood with the staples.

13. Perches beneath the entrance hole are not recommended, since they could encourage predators. Fit one if you like, however, using a natural twig inserted into a drilled hole.

14. Treat the finished nest box with a suitable preservative, carefully following the manufacturer's instructions and working in a well-ventilated area. Do this well in advance of hanging the box to allow the fumes to disperse. This also applies if you intend to paint the outside.

15. Site the box at least 6ft (2 metres) above the ground and away from direct sunshine, preferably among trees or shrubs. Put the box out many weeks before the breeding season to allow birds to become accustomed to its presence in their territory.

FIVE-BOARD
BENCH

From early times, the chair has always been a symbol of authority rather than merely something to sit on. From chieftains to chairmen, it has indicated status – and even today, from corporate body to village committee, the chairperson is recognized as being in charge. Until about the middle of the 16th century, chairs were a rarity; only the lord of the manor or the head of the family had one – everybody else made do with stools, benches or forms.

The most obvious difference between these "low-status" seats and chairs is that they are backless, but the difference between each one is not always so clear. A stool is a movable seat for one person, but if it is extended to accommodate more than one, it becomes either a bench or a form. Although these last two terms are often used synonymously, a bench was originally a substantial, fixed seat while a form is generally of lighter construction and is movable. In the British Parliament, the Members of Parliament sit on benches, and the more junior Members, who sit at the back, are known as back benchers. And it is from the use of the extended stool – the form – in the medieval school hall, where pupils sat in strict order of progress on the first, second or third form, that school classes or grades in Britain are in some places still known as "forms".

Stools and extended stools were constructed in different ways, from variations on the peg-leg type, like the milking

stool (see page 27), to the more elaborate, turned and carved "joyned" stool and bench. An early version was the trestle construction, some of these, not unlike the tables of the time, consisting of a board mounted on two solid end pieces which were braced in some way – sometimes centrally but, more usually, by side pieces. The ends might be either tenoned through the top and secured by wedging or made by a more simple method in which the five components are pegged, screwed or nailed together.

This type of bench (or form) was common across Europe and North America, and was most often made in pine and then painted. It was a popular piece of furniture for use both indoors and out. Its attraction lies in the ready availability of the raw material, the fact that it requires little in the way of woodworking skills, and only the simplest of tools are needed. The method of construction means that the bench can be made in an infinite variety of sizes and adapted to fulfil a number of functions, from the smallest child's stool to an extended bench suitable for seating several adults. By increasing its height, the bench naturally turns into a small table that, in style, is particularly suited for use in the garden or out on the porch. The dimensions given here are for a generous-sized two-seater, but it could easily be extended to seat three people or reduced to make a useful stool for one person.

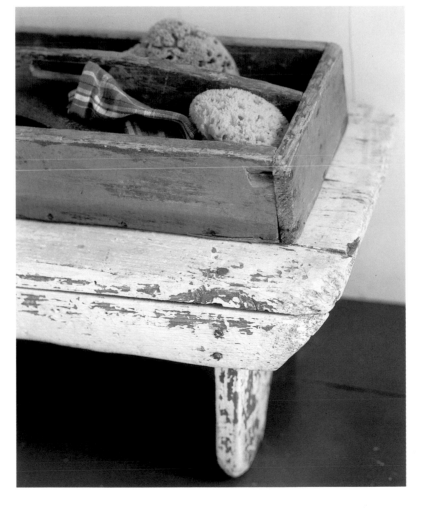

Left - THE VERSATILITY IN THE SIZE AND DESIGN OF THE FIVE-BOARD BENCH IS CLEARLY SEEN HERE. THIS COLLECTION OF PORCH BENCHES AND STOOLS ARE MOSTLY MADE OF PINE, THEIR WELL-WORN PAINTWORK TESTIMONY TO THEIR POPULARITY AND CONTINUING USE.

Above - A SMALL BENCH – PERHAPS ORIGINALLY DESIGNED AS A STOOL FOR A CHILD – HAS BEEN TURNED INTO A USEFUL LOW BENCH TABLE FOR A BATHROOM. THE ANTIQUE WOODEN CARRIER PERCHED ON TOP, ORIGINALLY A CARRIER FOR CUTLERY, SERVES AS A HOLD-ALL FOR BATHROOM ACCESSORIES.

ABILITY LEVEL: Novice

SIZE: 36 x 16⅞ x 12in (914 x 428 x 305mm)

MATERIALS: Pine or any hardwood

CUTTING LIST:
1 top
36 x 12 x ⅞in (914 x 305 x 22mm)

2 ends
16 x 10 x ⅞in (406 x 254 x 22mm)

2 sides
30 x 4 x ⅞in (762 x 102 x 22mm)

See template patterns on page 152 for cutting legs.

All measurements are given in inches, with the equivalents in millimetres indicated in brackets.

Note: If the bench is to used in the garden or on a porch, use waterproof glue when assembling the final pieces.

METHOD:

1. Select and prepare all the material using the dimensions given. If necessary, make up the 12in (305mm) widths by edge joining narrower boards (see page 141).

2. Cut out the shapes of the two end pieces (see page 152 for template pattern), or cut them out to a shape of your own design.

3. Cut the housings for the side rails as shown. Cut these to suit the exact dimensions of the side pieces in case these differ from those given in the cutting list. These housing joints, when well made and glued and nailed or screwed together, add considerably to the rigidity of the finished bench.

4. Now shape the ends of the side rails as shown and smooth off all sawn edges and sharp corners.

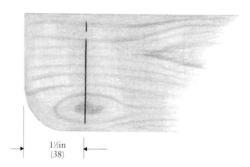

5. Mark pencil guide lines 1½in (38mm) in and square across on each end of the side rails as an aid to nailing or screwing. Note the 1in (25mm) overlap over the end pieces. This extra length reduces the risk of splitting when the side rails are joined to the end pieces.

6. Mark pencil guide lines square across the top, 4½in (114mm) in from each end and, parallel to the edge, 1½in (38mm) in from each edge. These, too, are an aid to nailing (or screwing).

7. The bench can be nailed together in traditional fashion, using oval or lost head nails. Take care not to split the wood, especially when fitting the side rails (see page 141 for advice). Punch the nail heads below the surface and fill the indentations.

8. As an alternative, you can join the bench together using countersunk screws. Drill and counterbore the holes to accommodate the screws and the wooden plugs glued in on top to conceal them (see page 141). If hardwood is being used, it must be screwed together.

9. Begin assembly by joining the side rails to the end pieces. Nail or screw as required. Apply glue first to strengthen the joints.

10. Check that the basic frame remains square and then wipe off surplus glue and leave it to dry.

11. Check that the top will fit correctly. Line up the pencil guide lines to give about a 4in (102mm) overhang at each end and a 1in (25mm) overhang over each side rail.

12. Using the pencil lines as a guide, nail or screw into both ends and side pieces. The nails or screws will hold better in the side rails than in the end grain of the end pieces.

13. Punch all nail heads below the surface and fill the indentations, or glue and plug the counterbored screw holes.

14. Remove the pencil marks and sand all surfaces clean. Round over all sharp edges, especially those on the top of the seat.

15. Finish according to your choice by clear varnishing, staining or painting (see pages 146-7 for advice on finishes). If the bench is to be used regularly outdoors, the application of a suitable wood preservative will prolong the life of the bench, especially if pine was used in its construction.

Below - OFFERING RELIEF FROM THE HEAT OF THE DAY, AND THE USUAL SEASONAL GARDEN CHORES, THIS SHADY BENCH IS SUFFICIENTLY INFORMAL IN DESIGN TO FIND FAVOUR IN ANY STYLE OF GARDEN.

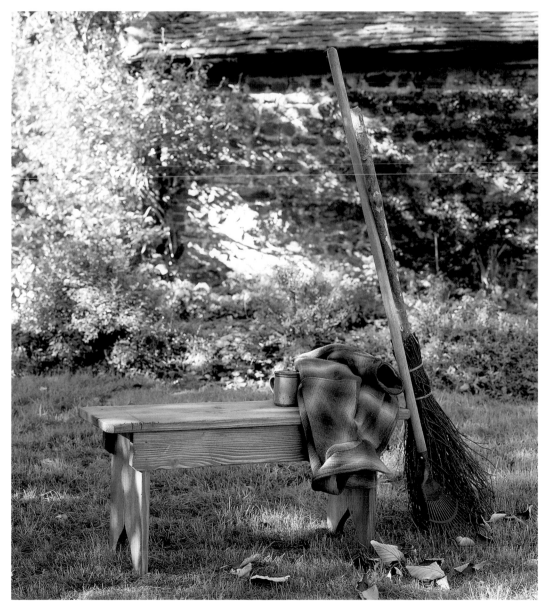

TRADITIONAL WHIRLIGIG

The easiest definition of whirligigs is that they are types of wind-driven toy. This, however, is a pretty inadequate definition, for they are much more than that. Part toy, part machine, they can vary from the very simple to the most complex; from a single moving object or figure to a whole orchestra (literally) of movement. Actuated by all types of mechanisms – by direct drive or through a series of cams and cranks – they can be driven by an assortment of different propeller designs, such as single blade, four-blade and multi-blade types. Whether they are whimsical weather vanes or windpowered wonderments, they are most often painted in bright colours. Their objective is entirely non-functional and their intention is simply to entertain and delight. Whirligigs were particularly popular in the United States during the 19th century, and they are now enjoying something of a revival: their origins, however, remain somewhat of a mystery. The name itself is derived from a combination of two Old Norse words: *whirl*, meaning to spin about, and *gig*, to turn or shake about. In the 15th century, whirligig, or "whirlygigge", was the name given to the toy that we now know as the spinning top, and also to the first merry-go-rounds at English village fairs. Folded paper pinwheels on sticks, sold as novelty toys at these fairs, and model or toy windmills, have also been known at one time or another as whirligigs, while the whirligig beetle is the common name in some localities for a whole family of flat-bodied water beetles that skim and whirl around on the surface of still water. It was also the name given to a type of revolving punishment cage used to hold criminals in the early part of the 15th century, and in the 19th century the now-common revolving office chair was called a whirligig long before it became known as the swivel chair. And the name has literary connections, too – William Shakespeare, in *Twelfth Night*, refers to "the whirligig of time". The American short story writer O. Henry (William Sydney Porter) called one of his books *Whirligigs*, an apt title for a collection of stories that twist and turn about and typically have surprise endings.

The colourful and animated wind-driven devices that we now call whirligigs may well have had an Asian ancestry, probably introduced from the Far East, perhaps by the Chinese, who are credited with the invention of both the windmill and the kite. Nothing is authentically documented, however. Settlers to North America no doubt brought many different designs with them, and, in the course of time, as with so many other items of culture, the figures they put on their whirligigs and the actions they performed took on a distinctive style that is unique to North America. In the past, whirligigs played an important role in the lives of hardworking country folk, providing both a recreational occupation for creative woodworking skills and an outlet for an obviously rich sense of humour.

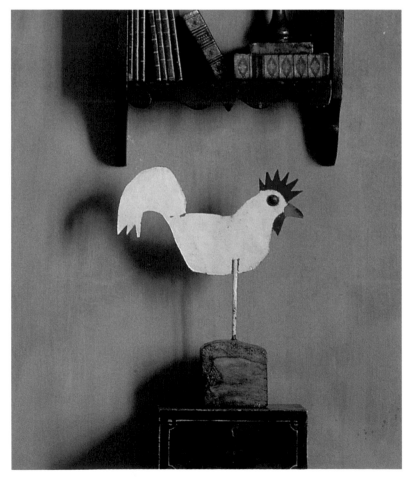

Above - THE WEATHER VANE IS A CLOSE RELATION OF THE WHIRLIGIG AND THE CROWING COCKEREL IS A FAVOURITE MOTIF IN THEIR MAKING. MADE FROM EITHER WOOD OR METAL, THESE BRIGHTLY PAINTED IMAGES ARE OFTEN USED DECORATIVELY IN THE COUNTRY-STYLE INTERIOR.

Right - THE THEME OF THIS COLOURFUL WHIRLIGIG, SEEN HERE AGAINST A BACKGROUND OF RIPENING MAIZE, IS "JACK CHOPPING WOOD". SUCH CHARACTERIZATION WAS A FEATURE OF MANY SUCH CONSTRUCTIONS, AND IT IS THIS THAT ENDEARS THEM TO MODERN COLLECTORS.

ABILITY LEVEL: Novice/Intermediate

SIZE: 20 x 18 x 1½in (508 x 457 x 38mm)

MATERIALS: Wood, waterproof plywood, metal

CUTTING LIST:
WOOD
1 platform
16 x 1 x ⅞in (406 x 25 x 22mm)

1 pivot block
3 x 1 x ⅞in (76 x 25 x 22mm)

1 drive shaft block
3 x 1½ x ⅞in (76 x 38 x 22mm)

1 propeller hub
3 x 3 x 1in (76 x 76 x 25mm)

4 pieces dowel
5 x ½in (127 x 12mm) diameter

1 small wooden bead

WATERPROOF PLYWOOD (OR WOOD)
Figure parts, axe, propeller blades, tail, chopping block
24 x 12 x ¼in (610 x 305 x 6mm)

METAL
1 piece threaded rod
5½ x ¼in (140 x 6mm) diameter

6 nuts and washers
¼in (6mm) diameter (to suit rod)

1 large flange washer
¼in x 1½in (6 x 38mm) OD

1 piece brass tubing
5 x 5⁄16in (127 x 8mm) OD

1 machine screw
2 x 3⁄16in (51 x 4mm) diameter

1 nut and 4 washers to suit machine screw

1 small screw eye, assorted nails, and screws for assembly

1 piece stiff wire for connecting rod

Notes: Use waterproof glue for assembly. The threaded rod (drive shaft) should run freely inside the brass tubing. The drive mechanism will need a drop of oil periodically; applying petroleum jelly to the drive shaft before assembly is a useful long-term precaution.

OD = outside diameter

See template patterns on page 154.

All measurements are given in inches, with the equivalents in millimetres indicated in brackets.

METHOD:

1. Using the full-sized templates on page 154, mark and cut out all of the parts for the figure. Cut one body, two waists, two legs, and two arms. Clean up all sawn edges.

2. Glue the arms and waists to the body, one either side as shown. Cramp the work until the glue is dry.

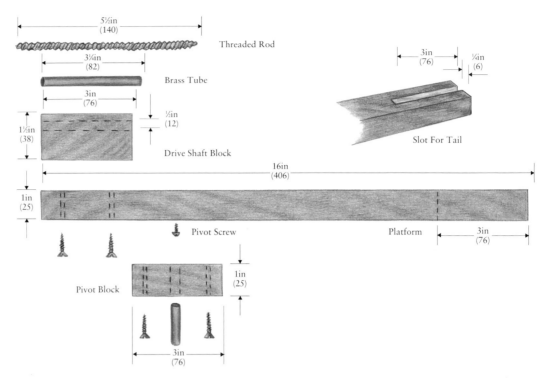

5½in (140) — Threaded Rod

3¼in (82)

Brass Tube

3in (76) — Drive Shaft Block

1½in (38)

½in (12)

3in (76) — ¼in (6) — Slot For Tail

16in (406)

1in (25) — Platform — 3in (76)

Pivot Screw

Pivot Block

1in (25)

3in (76)

3. When dry, drill the figure pivot hole through to clear the ³⁄₁₆in (4mm) machine screw. Align and drill corresponding holes through the legs at the same time.

4. Attach the legs to the figure using the machine screw, placing the washers as shown to reduce friction. Check that the movement is free and then put it aside until later.

5. Mark and cut out the remaining plywood/wood components using the templates on page 154. Clean up the sawn edges.

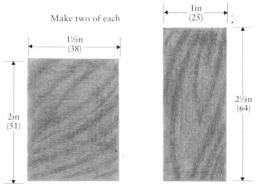

Make two of each

1in (25)

1½in (38)

2in (51)

2½in (64)

6. From the same material, cut out the chopping block parts and glue these together as shown on the right.

7. Cut the platform, drive shaft block, and pivot block to length. Make a ¼in (6mm) slot in one end of the platform for the tail to be fitted later. Then carefully drill a ⁵⁄₁₆in (8mm) diameter hole through the length of the drive shaft block.

8. Cut a 3¼in (82mm) length of the brass tubing and push this into the hole drilled in the drive shaft block, leaving equal amounts of tubing protruding from each end. File the ends of the tube smooth.

9. Drill a ⅛in (3mm) hole in the outer edge of the large flange washer for the connecting rod attachment. Place the threaded rod through the brass tube and assemble the washers and nuts, large flange washer, and lock nut, as shown. Don't overtighten. Test that the shaft rotates freely.

10. Drill a ⁵⁄₁₆in (8mm) diameter hole through the centre of the pivot block and push fit the remainder of the brass tubing into the hole to check that it fits.

11. Now screw and glue the two blocks to the platform in the positions shown on the opposite page. In order to reduce friction in the pivot block when it is mounted, position a round-headed screw in the underside of the platform, as shown above, before attaching the pivot block.

12. Glue and nail the figure to the platform in the position indicated. Screw the small eye into the back of the figure at the point shown, and then cut and bend the connecting rod wire, using the dimensions given as a guide only. Adjust as necessary. Put the small bead in place; this keeps the connecting rod clear of the end of the drive shaft. Attach the connecting rod to the flange washer and to the figure.

13. Test the movements of the drive shaft and figure and adjust the length of the connecting rod as necessary.

14. Make a deep V-shaped groove in the top of the chopping block and place it in position, without using glue, on the platform. Next, temporarily attach the axe between the figure's hands. Rotate the drive shaft and test the movement of the axe in relation to the chopping block. The axe should go partway into the groove without actually touching it. Adjust the positions of axe and block as necessary and then glue and pin them into place.

15. Make the four-bladed propeller as shown. The dimensions of the hub, propeller blades and other details are given with the templates (see page 154).

½in
(12)
diameter

16. It is easiest to drill the holes while the hub is still square. Carefully mark and drill right through the wood the ⁵⁄₁₆in (8mm) diameter centre hole, and then mark and drill to a depth of ¾in (19mm) the ½in (12mm) diameter propeller arm holes. Either cut the hub to shape or leave it square.

5in
(127)

17. After checking that the arm dowels fit in the holes drilled in the hub, cut the arm dowels halfway through, as shown. The flat surfaces formed by this shaping accommodate the propeller blades. The lower edges of the blades should not be closer than 3in (76mm) to the hub centre.

18. Glue the individual blades into position and secure them with small panel pins, taking care not to split the dowels (see page 141 for advice). Allow the glue to dry before going on to the next step.

19. Insert the arms into their respective holes in the hub, without using glue. Rotate the arms so that pairs of blades are at opposite angles of about 45° to each other on either side of the hub. Glue the arms into position. Test the propeller for balance, using a spare piece of rod or a suitable-sized nail as a free pivot. If one blade is heavy, it will always come to rest at the bottom. Remove surplus wood from the blades until the balance is correct. Then fit the propeller to the drive shaft and secure it with the nut and lock nut.

20. Fit, glue, and nail the tail into the tail slot already cut in the platform. The tail piece helps to keep the propeller facing into the wind. When the glue is dry, test the mechanism outside in the wind. It may be necessary to make minor adjustments to ensure smooth running.

21. If the whirligig is to be used outdoors, you must protect it with good-quality oil-based paint over a sound undercoat. Choose a realistic colour scheme, like the one shown on page 59, which uses earth colours and is in keeping with the style of the project. Make sure no paint is allowed to clog the working parts.

22. When the paint is dry, mount the whirligig on a suitable pivot, such as a steel rod or a nail driven into a stand or post.

23. The drive mechanism of the whirligig will need a drop of oil from time to time to ensure that it continues to work smoothly; applying a light grease (petroleum jelly) to the drive shaft before assembly is a useful long-term precaution.

Right - A FINE COLLECTION OF WHIRLIGIGS STANDS SENTINEL OVER THE PORCH OF A NORTH AMERICAN COUNTRY HOME IN NEW YORK STATE, EACH DEVICE PERCHED ON TOP OF ITS OWN POST TO CATCH THE SLIGHTEST BREEZE. THIS EXCELLENT LOCATION MEANS THEY CAN BE EASILY ENJOYED BY ANYONE VENTURING TO SIT OUTSIDE, AND PROVIDE COLOUR AND MOVEMENT. NOTE THE BRIGHT HUES THAT HAVE BEEN USED FOR THEIR DECORATION – THERE IS NO NEED TO LIMIT YOURSELF TO THE MORE SOBER EARTH COLOURS IF BRIGHT AND CHEERFUL IS WHAT YOU WANT. THE RESULT WILL STILL BE AUTHENTIC.

ROCKING CHAIR

Perhaps more than any other single item of household furniture, the rocking chair evokes the strongest feeling of the past and the comfort of country living. The origin of the rocking chair is obscure but it seems to have appeared throughout Europe and North America towards the end of the 18th century. In America, rocking chairs became extremely popular, especially for after dinner relaxation, and they were apparently given the name "digestive chairs". However, in Victorian England, they were considered "socially unacceptable" and were only approved of on medical grounds – presumably as an aid to digestion!

Their acceptance and popularity in America led to the development of specially designed rocking chairs such as the Boston Rocker, and the Shaker communities also made many of their chairs to rock. The much-exported Thonet range of bentwood furniture from Austria included several quite elaborate rocking chairs in which the rockers were an integral part of the construction. In Britain, there appears to have been few, if any, chairs made specifically for rocking. Instead, during the late 19th century, chairs which were normally stationary could have rockers fitted to them at the request of the purchaser and trade catalogues of the period offered to fit rockers for the cost of an extra shilling.

To understand the small size of the rocking chair on the left of this picture one has to appreciate the extent to which domestic living has changed over the centuries. From ancient times family life concentrated around the hearth and the fireplace was the principle source of light as well as heat; it was where people cooked, ate, talked and made music. Because the fire was at a low level, so chair seat heights were correspondingly low, and because there was often a need to accommodate as many people as possible around the fire, chairs were designed to take up minimum space. Later, the table replaced the hearth as the domestic gathering point. As a result, chair seat heights were raised to allow for sitting at the table and in time chairs became both taller and bulkier. However, small, hearth culture chairs are still found throughout Europe and North America. The following project explains how to make a small rocking chair.

Left - THE FURNITURE ON THIS PORCH INCLUDES THE SMALL ROCKING CHAIR DESCRIBED IN THE PROJECT. THE BENTWOOD CHAIRS, COMMONLY MADE IN THE SOUTHERN UNITED STATES, ARE MADE FROM GREEN (UNSEASONED), SUPPLE, FAST-GROWING WOODS SUCH AS WILLOW AND COTTONWOOD.

ABILITY LEVEL: Intermediate

SIZE: 34 x 16 x 16in (863 x 406 x 406mm)

MATERIALS: Ash, Beech, Maple

CUTTING LIST:

2 back uprights
31 x 2 x 1¼in (787 x 51 x 32mm)

2 front legs
14 x 2 x 1¼in (355 x 51 x 32mm)

(Cut the 2 back uprights and 2 front legs from 2 pieces of wood: 31 x 5 x 1¼in/ 787 x 127 x 32mm)

2 seat rails
15 x 2 x 1in (380 x 50 x 25mm)

7 stretcher rails
15 x 1⅛ x 1⅛in (381 x 28 x 28mm)

1 back rail
15 x 1½ x 1in (381 x 38 x 25mm)

1 comb (cut from 1 piece)
16 x 4 x 3in (406 x 101 x 76mm)

1 seat (made from 3 pieces)
17 x 4 x 1in (431 x 101 x 25mm)

2 rockers (cut from 1 piece)
30 x 6 x 1½in (762 x 152 x 38mm)

See template patterns on page 155 for comb, seat and rockers.

All measurements given in inches, with the equivalents in millimetres indicated in brackets.

METHOD:

Construction of this chair is simplified if the sequence of making two separate side "units" and then joining these together with cross rails is followed.

1. Cut out the two back uprights (see pattern page 155, ⅓rd actual size). Clean up sawn surfaces: leave rectangular below seat level; above, smooth over the outside edges only and round the top to 1in (25mm) diameter.

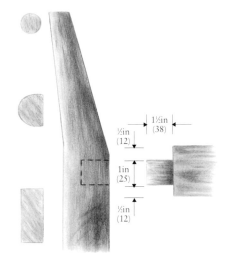

2. Make the two front legs (see pattern on page 155) and clean up sawn surfaces.

3. Mark out and cut mortises for the seat rails in the back uprights and front legs (see page 144 for mortise and tenon joint).

4. Check that the seat rails are of correct and equal length; mark out and cut tenons to fit mortises. Check for a snug fit.

5. Make four round side stretcher rails to length and 1in (25mm) diameter by turning or by any other means. Form ¾in (19mm) diameter tenon joints at each end.

6. Mark the position of the stretcher rails on the inside edges of the front legs and leg portion of the back uprights. Drill these joint sockets ¾in (19mm) diameter and 1¼in (32mm) deep.

7. Test fit the side stretcher rails individually to make sure that they fit properly into the leg sockets.

8. Assemble the dry (unglued) back uprights, front legs, seat rails and side stretcher rails to make two separate side "units".

9. Cut out a pair of rockers (see pattern on page 155). Clean up sawn surfaces.

10. With the side "units" lying on a flat surface, place a rocker on to each as shown, and mark the top curve of the rocker on the bottom end of each leg. Also mark the position of mortises for leg tenons on each rocker.

11. Cut leg mortises into each rocker. Keep the joint vertical to a flat surface and not to the rocker surface.

12. Mark out and cut leg tenons, scribing the shoulder of each joint to the marked line (see step 10) to obtain a close fit with the top surface of the rocker.

13. Check the fit of the tenons into the mortises in the rockers. Disassemble for the next stages.

14. Make 3 round cross stretcher rails to length and 1in (25mm) diameter (see page 138 for advice on shaping). Form ¾in (19mm) round tenon joints at each end.

15. Mark out the position of these rails on the outside surfaces of the legs and drill through at ¾in (19mm). Test fit the rails.

16. Mark out the position of the mortises in the back uprights for the back cross rail. Cut these mortises.

17. Mark out and cut the stub tenons on the ends of the back cross rail. Hollow the front surface of the rail for added comfort, as shown.

18. Cut out the comb to the pattern (see page 155). Clean up sawn surfaces, but to make drilling easier in the next step, leave rounding over the top edge and ends until after the joint sockets have been made.

19. Temporarily assemble the back uprights and cross rails to check the width apart of the top round tenons. Mark this measurement on the underside of the comb and drill these joint sockets ¾in (19mm) and 1in (25mm) deep.

20. Form a ¾in (19mm) shouldered round tenon on top of each back upright and try the comb for a good fit.

21. Make up the seat to the pattern from pieces which may be edge glued together or left separate. Round over the front edge.

22. To assemble the chair: begin by gluing and assembling the two side "units", including the rockers. Secure the joints by pegging (see page 145).

23. Join the two side "units" together by adding the cross rails. Note that these go through the back uprights and front legs. Secure by pegging and cut joints flush, if they are protruding.

24. Fit the comb on to the back upright tenons.

25. Fit the seat boards by nailing or screwing into the side seat rails. Punch nails or countersink screw below the surface and fill the indentations.

26. The chair may be finished by any of the methods described on pages 146-7.

RUSTIC
CHAIR

Wherever there is thriving woodland, there you will find young sapling trees. These are the result of natural regeneration, regrowth after a forest fire perhaps, or the natural cycle of recovery following the clearance of mature trees by managed felling. In some woodland management systems, coppicing – the cutting of mature trees to encourage multi-stemmed regrowth – is a productive means of producing wood on a regular crop basis. Historically, these straight stems have been used in a variety of ways.

In the past, as well as on a small scale today, young tree stems were used for fencing, barn partitions, sheep hurdles, and fodder racks, and it was but a short step to use this versatile material for simple, rustic furniture. Much the same methods of construction were employed – round tenons whittled on the end of round rails and secured into holes bored into joining pieces or, where components crossed each other, bound with cords or strips of bark. Nails might sometimes be used, but these were not always available and were expensive to buy when they were. Basic furniture, such as beds, tables, stools, and chairs, were all made in this way, and some folk styles today in Eastern Europe, Scandinavia, and North America still use similar forms of construction.

It was in the newly established colonies of 17th-century North America that this furniture really proliferated. Virgin forests provided an abundance of materials for building purposes, and the early pioneers were quick to take advantage of such a convenient and seemingly endless supply of timber. The first furniture would have been made from this same source, and it served its purpose well until replaced or relegated to a secondary role, usually as garden furniture, by the requirements of fashion and social change.

Interestingly, it is as the result of this social change and the growing pressures of urbanization that a revival of interest in the rustic furniture style has taken place. The organic feel of the style, its tactile surfaces, and the decorative qualities of the wood and the way it is used have an instant aesthetic appeal and, together with its simplicity, provides the ideal complement to a back-to-nature decor.

Right - A GALLERY OF RUSTIC-STYLE CHAIRS FOR USE IN THE GARDEN OR ON A COUNTRY PORCH. ALL THE CHAIRS SHOWN HERE ARE NORTH AMERICAN EXCEPT FOR THE ONE CENTRE TOP. THIS WAS MADE BY THE AUTHOR AND DETAILS OF ITS CONSTRUCTION ARE GIVEN IN THE PROJECT THAT FOLLOWS.

ABILITY LEVEL: Intermediate

SIZE: 43 x 20 x 18in (1092 x 508 x 457mm)

MATERIALS: Young growth of Hazel, Birch, or Ash

CUTTING LIST:
2 back uprights
43 x 2in (1092 x 51mm) diameter

2 front uprights
28 x 2in (711 x 51mm) diameter

2 back rails
19 x 1½in (483 x 38mm) diameter

2 front rails
19 x 1½in (483 x 38mm) diameter

4 side rails
18 x 1½in (457 x 38mm) diameter

2 arms
22 x 1¾in (559 x 44mm) diameter

1 comb
23 x 1¾in (584 x 44mm) diameter

6 back sticks
24 x 1in (610 x 25mm) diameter

3 "H" pieces
10 x 1in (254 x 25mm) diameter

10 seat pieces
21½ x 1½in (546 x 38mm) diameter

Note: Diameters are approximate only and are given as a guide when gathering materials. Initially, cut pieces generously overlength and allow them to season (dry) before using them. The ends will probably split during the drying process.

All measurements are given in inches, with the equivalents in millimetres indicated in brackets.

Note: If the chair is to be used in the garden or on the porch, use waterproof glue when assembling the final pieces.

METHOD:

1. Select material according to its length and diameter. Choose back uprights that have a slight backward curve; all other pieces should be as straight as possible. When all pieces are thoroughly seasoned, cut everything to length. Remove the bark if you prefer, using a drawknife.

2. The chair is made in the form of two "ladders", back and front, of different lengths, joined together using side rails. This greatly simplifies the construction process. First, shape the top ends of both back uprights and front to form round tenons of 1in (25mm) diameter. These are for the back comb and arms, respectively. Use a chisel, abrasives, drawknife or spokeshave to form the tenons.

3. Now mark and drill the joint sockets in the two back uprights to accommodate the two back rails. Do the same in the front uprights for the two front rails. Drill these sockets to a depth and diameter of 1in (25mm). Then shape the ends of the back and front rails to form round tenons, 1in (25mm) in diameter, to fit the drilled sockets.

4. Assemble the front and back "ladders", without using glue, by fitting the rails into the uprights. Make sure the joints go in to their full depth. Mark the component pieces for their correct positions. Disassemble.

5. Mark the positions of the side rails on the back and front uprights and drill these to a depth and diameter of 1in (25mm), and at right angles to those previously drilled.

6. Now mark and drill the sockets to hold the arms. These angle slightly upward, as shown, to allow for the slope of the arms. Next, shape the ends of the side rails (see step 3) to form 1in (25mm) diameter tenons. Test fit rails in their respective sockets, making sure they enter to their full depth.

7. Reassemble the front and back "ladders", without gluing. Join these to the side rails to make the basic chair frame. Check that the chair stands without rocking. If necessary, use a soft mallet to tap the joints fully home.

8. Now mark the positions of the other components in the following order, although the measurements given are only a guide and may differ from chair to chair.

9. First, shape the joint end of each of the arms to a diameter of 1in (25mm) and fit them into their previously drilled sockets in the back uprights. Make sure they enter to their full depth and, while they are in place, mark the positions for drilling the front arm sockets to fit the tenons already made on the top of each front upright. Next, drill the arms at the marked positions to a depth and diameter of 1in (25mm) and test fit the components. Drill these sockets at a slight angle to allow for the slope of the arms. Round over or bevel the front end of each arm.

10. Mark the position of the sockets in the back comb to fit the tenons on the top of each back upright. Drill these to a depth and diameter of 1in (25mm) and test fit the components. Round over or bevel the ends.

11. Mark the positions of the sockets for the six back sticks on the top surface of the back rail and the underside of the back comb. Space these out equally, about 2½in (64mm) apart, but check this on your own chair.

12. Mark the position of the vertical pieces of the front "H" on the top and bottom front rails, at the places shown. Disassemble basic frame. Drill back stick sockets to a diameter of ⅝in (16mm) and a depth of ¾in (19mm).

13. Drill the front "H" sockets in the top and bottom front rails, to a diameter of ⅝in

(16mm) and a depth of ¾in (19mm). Also drill the sockets for the cross piece.

14. Shape the ends of the back sticks to form ⅝in (16mm) diameter round tenons. Test these in turn for fit in the drilled sockets. Then assemble the entire back "ladder", without gluing. Check for fit and square.

15. Shape the ends of the "H" pieces and try them individually for fit in the previously drilled sockets. Some adjustment of length may be needed. Without gluing, fit the front "H" into the front rails, assemble the entire front "ladder" and check for fit and square.

16. Without gluing, join the front and back "ladders" together with the side rails and put the arms into position. Check the complete chair goes together properly, then disassemble ready for gluing. First, glue together the back "ladder" and the front "ladder". Check that all joints fit to their full depth and that all is square. Add the side rails, then the arms. Make sure the joints fit to their full depth. Check the assembled chair stands upright on a level surface. You may want to peg the arms and the top front and top side rails (see page 145) for extra strength.

17. The seat consists of several separate pieces placed side by side across the side seat rails, their tops level with the top front rail. Nail these into place, using a single oval or lost head nail at each end. To avoid splitting the wood, drill a small hole in each piece first, then punch the nail heads below the surface.

18. Give the completed chair an oil finish or treat it with two or three coats of thinned polyurethane varnish. The use of a suitable wood preservative is recommended (see pages 146-7 for advice on finishes).

Much of the appeal of the country kitchen lies in its integrity and functional simplicity and in the kitchen's symbolic role as the heart of the house. Represented by strong, warm, time-toned colours and textures, everything is as well made as it is well used. There is little pretence of conformity, and you will find few "rules" regarding style.

Wood frequently predominated in the kitchen interiors of old, for it was discovered long ago that wood was the material most suited to the purpose. Furniture, implements, utensils, even the very fabric of the walls and ceiling, were often made entirely from wood. Today a fairly authentic note can be achieved by using tongue-and-groove planking on walls, and possibly the ceiling, too. Paint it in a suitable "earth" colour, and you have the ideal backdrop for a country-style kitchen. Choose furniture that continues the theme – for example, a scrubbed pine table, a selection of simply constructed chairs, mix-and-match cupboards and a basic dresser. Hang cheerful gingham or checked curtains at the window, then decorate the walls and dresser with an eclectic mixture of old and new kitchenware, rural artefacts and anything else that appeals.

THE RURAL KITCHEN

In contrast to the crowded, gadget-packed kitchens we are familiar with today, it is difficult to imagine just how sparsely furnished and equipped were the kitchens of our ancestors. In those times, the kitchen of a farm labourer, for example, would have contained little more than a sturdy table for food preparation, supplemented by a storage cupboard and perhaps a wall-hung pot shelf. Until the advent of the separate dining room, sometime in the 18th century, all meals would have been taken at the kitchen table, too, and for this purpose a few chairs or a bench would have been provided. In homes where there were large families, far more common than it is today, it is unlikely there would even have been enough seats to go around, and some, usually the younger family members, would have eaten their food standing up or squatting on the floor.

Central to the kitchen was the fireplace or open hearth, with the fire often the only source of heat and the principal source of light after sunset. Since it was vital to the wellbeing and comfort of the entire household, laying the fire was the first task every morning.

Right Below & Left - PLAIN WOODEN BENCHES PROVIDE USEFUL SEATING AT THE TABLE IN THE KITCHEN OR DINING ROOM AND SAVE SPACE, TOO. THE TWO BENCHES SHOWN HERE ARE COUNTRY-MADE, THEIR LEGS BRACED FOR STRENGTH IN DIFFERENT BUT EQUALLY SUPPORTIVE WAYS.

Right - PRODUCE FROM THE GARDEN, HUNG TO DRY FROM A RACK, AND A DEC-ORATIVE BESOM BROOM PROPPED IN A CORNER BRING A TOUCH OF THE OUTDOORS TO THIS MODERN COUNTRY-STYLE KITCHEN WITH ITS NATURAL WOOD TONES AND SIMPLY DESIGNED FURNITURE.

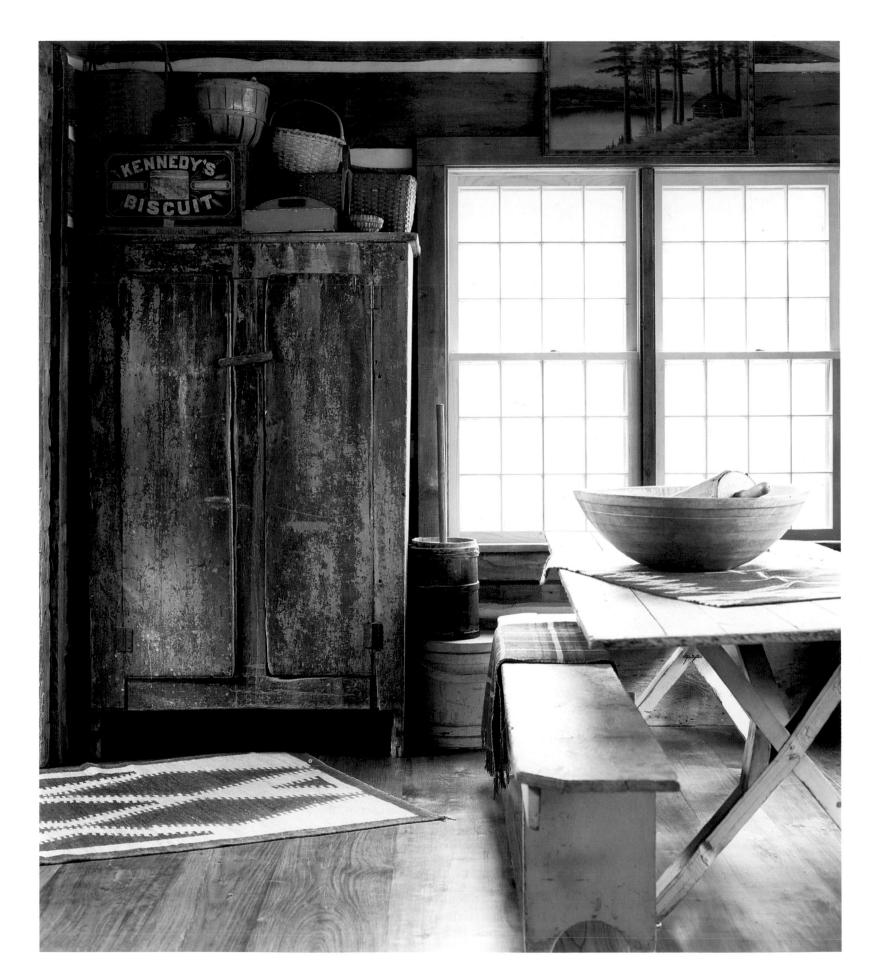

When the log cabins of the early American settlers were being built, the large stone fireplace and chimney were the first elements of the building to be constructed, and the remainder of the building was then put up around them.

All cooking was done in, on, or over an open fire, and while it was fuelled by wood, hearths and cooking methods remained largely unchanged for centuries. It was not until the 19th century, when coal became widely available, that the hearth changed considerably. Because coal needs a constant supply of air in order to burn properly, it has to be contained in some type of raised iron basket or grate in order to create a better draught. This, in turn, led to the introduction of various types of enclosed, cast-iron constructions known as kitchen ranges, or stoves. These provided a means of cooking not only directly over the fire itself but also, indirectly, on a metal hot-plate, or hob. An oven was also provided as well as a side or back boiler, which supplied hot water. Made to fit into the space previously occupied by the old hearths, kitchen ranges were literally bricked into the open fireplaces, which, gradually, fell out of favour, except in the poorest or most isolated of rural households.

Smaller, freestanding kitchen ranges, known as portable stoves, which were supported on four legs and had an iron pipe to act as a flue, were an American innovation. It was not until the Great Exhibition in London, England, in 1851 that these portable stoves became available in Britain. These stoves may be seen as the inspiration of the now-ubiquitous Aga cooker – an invention of the Nobel Prize winner Dr Gustav Dalen in the 1920s. Since then, and certainly today, the Aga has come to embody the very essence of the modern country kitchen.

TABLE DESIGNS

The cottages and larger houses of the more prosperous rural dwellers – those of a skilled tradesman, shopkeeper, or tenant farmer, for example – would have had a sizeable kitchen-cum-dining room and some additional pieces of furniture. With more space available, there would have been room for a big table and, no doubt, enough seats for everybody in the family. Some of these early kitchen/dining tables were really massive affairs, sturdily built to last through several generations of use, and abuse. Some of these tables, in fact, are still with us today (together with many more reproductions of varying quality), which testifies to their fitness of purpose and the excellence of their construction.

Large numbers of kitchen/dining tables had tops made from pine, while harder timbers, such as oak and elm, were used in the construction of the legs and underframe. These pine tops, especially those of some early American tables, were often made from a single piece of wood. With the abundant supply of virgin forest at their

Above - GOOD, EASILY ACCESSIBLE STORAGE IS AN ESSENTIAL INGREDIENT IN THE WELL-RUN KITCHEN. THIS LARGE, BUILT-IN WOODEN DRESSER OFFERS EVERYTHING FROM DEEP DRAWERS AND ENCLOSED AND GLAZED CUPBOARDS TO A HANDY THREE-TIER PLATE RACK.

Left - THE SIMPLICITY OF WIDE, BARE FLOORBOARDS, A PLAIN WOODEN BENCH, A BASIC TRESTLE TABLE AND A LARGE AND USEFUL CUPBOARD CONTRAST STRIKINGLY WITH THE ELEGANT 18TH-CENTURY SASH WINDOWS IN THIS AMERICAN KITCHEN. THE WOVEN RUG AND MATS ADD A WELCOME TOUCH OF COLOUR.

disposal, it was not uncommon for the early settler to find trees of considerable girth, trees that yielded boards between 3 and 4 feet (more than 1 metre) in width.

Like all board material used at that time, the timber would have been laboriously sawn by hand. The technique employed was known as pit-sawing. The saw used for this was more than 6 feet (2 metres) in length and two men were needed to operate it. With the log to be sawn secured lengthwise over a pit dug in the ground (or sometimes supported on a very heavy framework raised above it), one man stood on top of the log, and the other below it. Between them, they pushed and pulled the saw progressively through the log. It was hard work, and sweat and sawdust fell freely until the entire log was converted into usable boards. Knowing about and appreciating the toil required in obtaining sawn boards by this method are part of what makes old furniture so very special.

The warmth of wood is an invitation to conviviality and a wooden table, unadorned with cloth or covers, is the perfect setting for good food. Tables vary enormously in design and regional features, especially in the type of underframe used. Among the earliest are those that developed from a separate board-and-trestle arrangement, which consisted of a pair of shaped trestles linked together with a cross-member tenoned through and secured with wedges. Benches frequently utilize this type of construction, too. Similar, but more lightly made table supports, common in Shaker furniture, are known as "I" trestles. The so-called "joyned", or frame-jointed, table is familiar to us as the type with a leg at each corner. There are many variations of this latter type, with either square or lathe-turned legs.

One design of table, which originated with the early American settlers, is the sawbuck, or "X"-frame, table. This is a type of trestle arrangement, and when you find one that is well made with cross-lapped joints, you have a very durable table support. In some parts of the country, it is known as the 10-dollar table because its "X" shape is the same as the Roman numeral for the number 10.

Tables designed to extend in size were often of the gate-leg type, a popular design on both sides of the Atlantic. The Pembroke style, which has long side flaps supported on hinged wooden brackets, was

Top Left - MODERN FURNITURE IS SKILFULLY INTEGRATED INTO THIS RESTORED AMERICAN KITCHEN. THE HANDMADE PINE CUPBOARDS, DESIGNED TO ACCOMMODATE A MODERN COOKERY HOB AND OTHER APPLIANCES, BLEND WELL WITH THE ORIGINAL BARE WOODEN FLOORBOARDS. THE TALL STOOL IS MODERN, TOO.

Below Left - THE ADJOINING DINING ROOM IS CLEVERLY KEPT APART FROM THE KITCHEN BY A LOW WOODEN PARTITION, PROVIDING A DISTINCTIVELY SEPARATE EATING AREA WHILE KEEPING EVERYTHING AS OPEN AS POSSIBLE.

Right - THE RUSTIC CHARM OF THIS ROOM LIES IN THE FREEDOM OF ITS COLOURFUL CLUTTER, AND THE MIXTURE OF PLAIN AND PAINTED WOODEN PIECES.

also popular. Various small tables were found to be useful both in the kitchen/dining room and elsewhere in the house. Among these were the different designs of side table that evolved as well as what are now generally known as tavern tables. These tavern tables can be found with round, square, and, occasionally, oval tops.

SEATING SOLUTIONS
An assortment of chairs, as well as benches, can be used to provide seating around a table. Well-used Windsors, in many different styles, can be found made from such woods as ash or yew. The saddled elm seats of older Windsors portray the grain of a hundred years of growth, and their polished patina an additional hundred years of use. Arranged with care in a room they seem to glow a mellow welcome in the flicker of a log fire or in the candle light of an intimate evening meal. Fine ladderbacks, English Gimson, or American Shaker – dark-stained or honey-coloured natural ash, beech, or hickory – add that authentic touch of rural crafts. With their hand-woven cane or rush seats and simple shapes, these are the first true chairs of the countryside.

Early chair makers chose their wood with particular care, cleaving it along the grain in order to retain its fibrous strength, and then shaping it by hand or with simple foot-operated lathes. To make the curved parts, the wood was first steamed and then bent into shape while it was still pliable. The components were then jointed and assembled tight – this, and the juxtaposition of opposing components, constituted the inherent tension that held the finished chair together indefinitely. Many of the chairs made in this way during the 19th century are still in serviceable

use today, but good examples are less easy to find and so often fetch a high price in antique shops and auctions. But mass-produced reproductions abound, some better than others. However, the best are still the ones that have been made by craftsmen following traditional methods of production. A small but growing number of makers produce chairs in this manner, having studied the old techniques and ways of working. Many chair makers work alone, and most create authentic country chairs in a variety of designs, which can then be given either a modern, usually clear finish, or an antique stained and distressed appearance.

DRESSERS
In large kitchen/dining rooms, a dresser of some type would have held pride of place. The word "dresser" is Norman French in origin, coming from *dressour*, which is the verb "to dress", in the sense of "to prepare". The dresser is a development of the highly ornate, medieval court cupboard, which was primarily used to display the splendour of the wealthy owner's "plate". It is also a close relative of the sideboard of the same and later periods. The dresser reappeared again in the early 17th century, but this time as a piece of furniture associated more with the country kitchen or dining room than the baronial hall.

At this time, the dresser was little more than a side table on which food was prepared, or dressed, in readiness for cooking or for serving at the dining table. Some were fitted with drawers below the work top and most stood on turned legs. A positive step towards the kitchen dresser as we know it today took place in about 1690, when a low backboard was added to the dresser top and, on the wall behind, a row of shelves was fixed to serve as a plate rack. The "plate" now was not of gold and silver,

however, as in medieval times, but of pewter and earthenware and, later, blue-and-white willow-pattern pottery.

From these very mixed beginnings, a number of distinct regional styles of dresser emerged – most of them lumped together today, quite incorrectly, under the one general term of Welsh dresser. Of the several different styles, the one closest to the 18th-century original is that correctly known as the pot-board dresser. This piece of furniture has the dresser top supporting a plain rack of shelves with shaped side supports and a moulded cornice. Below the top are two or more drawers supported underneath by turned legs. These legs are joined together at floor level by way of a wide, continuous shelf – the pot board. Another type of dresser has its lower section below the drawers fitted with more shelves and enclosed by doors to form two or three cupboards. A third type has two cupboards and a central opening, or knee hole, while the Irish coop dresser incorporates an enclosed space with a slatted wooden front in which it was the custom to keep laying hens – the warmth indoors encouraged the hens to continue laying eggs during the winter months.

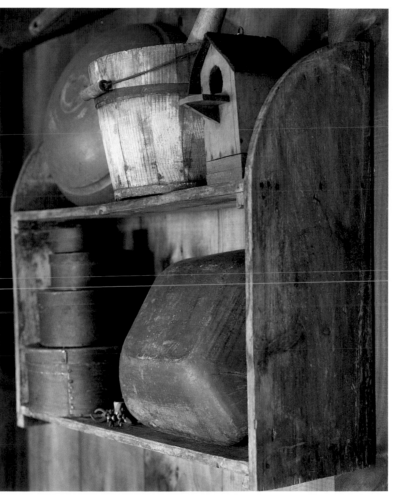

Whatever its type or style, the kitchen dresser is a much-used and much-loved piece of furniture. It provides an aesthetic as well as a decorative focal point while, at the same time, providing a functional storage and display space in the kitchen or dining room. The Scotsman John Claudius Loudon, author of *Encyclopaedia of Cottage, Farm and Villa Architecture and Furniture*, published in 1833, says that: ". . . dressers are essential to every kitchen, but more especially to the cottager, to whom they serve both as dresser and sideboard. They are generally well made of deal [pine] by local joiners and seldom painted, it being the pride of good housewives, in most parts of England, to keep the boards of which they are composed as white as snow by frequently scouring them with fine sand."

UTENSILS, IMPLEMENTS, AND CONTAINERS

In the past, the use of wood in the kitchen/dining room area was not restricted to furniture alone – it was also used extensively for most of the utensils and implements employed in the preparation of food. With the exception of an iron cooking pot or two and a few metal knives, almost everything else in daily use in the kitchen – spoons, ladles, platters and plates, bowls, rolling pins, and cutting boards – were fashioned from wood, either home made or bought from local craftsmen. Their makers shared a common knowledge about which wood to use and how to make each particular item.

Before designers had the opportunity to become obsessed with plastics, aluminium, and stainless steel, wood was also used in a variety of other ways, notably for containers and "smallware" of all descriptions. Smallware is an imprecise term covering such things as boxes, spoon racks, dough troughs, tubs, and buckets. Some of these wooden objects were simply, often crudely, made; others, however, displayed a great deal of innate skill and reveal much about their makers. Examples of smallware include spoons and ladles, which, although strictly utilitarian in purpose, frequently have such graceful shapes and lines that they are a joy to behold and to touch and use.

Left - CONTAINERS OF ALL KINDS, FOR STORAGE, MIXING AND SERVING, ARE IMPORTANT PIECES OF EQUIPMENT IN ANY KITCHEN, AND IN THE PAST THESE WERE OFTEN MADE FROM WOOD AND EITHER LEFT PLAIN OR PAINTED. THE SELECTION SHOWN ON THE LEFT REPRESENTS YEARS OF ENJOYABLE COLLECTING BY ONE AMERICAN COOK, WITH AN EYE TO THEIR BEAUTY AS WELL AS THEIR USEFULNESS.

Above - AN OVERLADEN STORAGE SHELF HOLDS A VARIETY OF OLD WOODEN CONTAINERS: A LARGE BRIGHT RED BOWL, A COOPERED PAIL, FOUR ROUND BOXES IN DIMINISHING DIAMETERS, AND AN UPTURNED RECTANGULAR DOUGH BOWL PAINTED BLUE. SOMEWHAT OUT OF OF PLACE AMONG THESE KITCHEN ITEMS, A PAINTED NEST BOX WAITS FOR THE NEXT BREEDING SEASON.

Containers and vessels for a wide range of household applications are sometimes ingenious in their construction. Round and oval boxes, for example, created from thin pieces of maple, birch, or cherry wood, required special skills to make. Steamed to make the wood pliable, and then bent to make the right shape on formers/forms, these boxes have carefully riveted seams. The best examples of these boxes were fashioned with distinctive and delicately shaped overlapping "fingers", secured with copper rivets at the joint. Decorative but practical, too, the technique of leaving spaces between the fingers allowed the thin, wooden sides to shrink or swell with any changes in humidity, so minimizing the risk of the box warping or splitting, as was common with straight-jointed boxes. This style of traditional box was adopted and perfected by the various Shaker communities in North America. These storage boxes were made in a range of sizes to stack tidily one on top of the other, combining neatness and utility with a religious undertone: piled in this way, the boxes also represented the "stairs to heaven", which every Shaker yearned to climb. The boxes were often painted in earth colours such as a buttermilk yellow, soft brick red or blueberry. Perhaps more than any other object, they have become symbolic of the Shaker dedication to fine craftsmanship.

Containers such as buckets, tubs, milk churns, and anything else that needed to hold liquids, were made by coopers. With great skill, these craftsmen shaped and fitted together the staves from which the vessels were constructed. Held in place by precisely made wooden or metal hoops, the individual staves were so well fitted that, when complete, the container was both watertight and durable. These items now mostly serve a purely decorative function in the modern country-style kitchen. If you want to give old wooden buckets and tubs a more useful life, use them as containers for plants. Always put a drip tray in the bottom and keep the plant in its original pot so that water can drain away.

In modern homes, you can inject something of the country mood into your surroundings through the judicious use of similar wooden objects. Wood is a timeless, sympathetic material, infinitely adaptable, and capable of blending comfortably with most other materials, fabrics, and pottery, be they old or new. Above all, wood is simply a pleasure to live with.

Right - The range of utensils used in the kitchen is enormous, even today. The earliest implements were always made of wood, and even when metal came into widespread use for cutlery and other kitchenware, a wooden handle was often still preferred. Spoons and spatulas of all shapes and sizes are still in everyday use (*Top Left*). Wooden clothes pegs (*Bottom Centre*) were cheaply made by splitting twigs and binding them with a strip of tin. The half-moon cutters (*Bottom Right*) are excellent for finely chopping vegetables and herbs.

SPOON RACK &
SPOONS

The simple wooden spoon, one of the earliest kitchen implements, is still used today by the modern cook and it is, in fact, often recommended when mixing ingredients in proprietary non-stick cookware. The surfaces of these containers would soon become abraded by a metal mixing spoon. However, wooden spoons sold in stores today are mere shadows of what they once were. Not only are they all pretty well standardized and mass-produced, they are also flat and uninteresting, suitable only for the stirring purpose for which they are recommended.

A wooden spoon was once an item of great importance in both town and country households, where it was used not only in the preparation of food but also, together with a pointed knife (forks came on the scene much later), for eating it. Antique examples show a wonderful and truly diverse variety of shapes and sizes – long handles, short handles, some straight and others curved, spoons with large bowls, small bowls, but almost always deep bowls. Spoons in those days were made to hold a generous helping of thick stew, soup or broth – not the timid, polite quantities favoured in countries where a high percentage of the population is at any one time embarking on some form of diet.

All these spoons were made by hand, and the carving of them was carried out by fulltime spoon carvers or by others as a pastime in the long winter evenings. Most spoons were strictly for utilitarian purposes, but others were highly ornate,

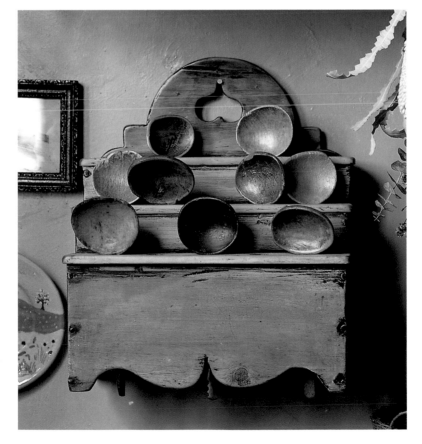

even fanciful. These decorated examples were often given by their makers as a token of affection to a sweetheart. Love spoons, as these later came to be called, date back three centuries or more. Originally, it seems, they were intended to be used by the recipient, but as the carving became more and more elaborate, they took on a purely symbolic role. A spoon carved with a single heart indicated "I love you", while an eye meant "I like what I see". To signify mutual love, a spoon would be carved with two bowls, or two spoons would be joined together by a linked chain.

In Wales, particularly, love spoons are still made for the tourist trade, but they have none of the history or the romance of the genuine articles. Antique love spoons are much collected these days. Since they were regarded as treasured possessions, spoons (and knives, too) were, accordingly, generally well looked after. While knives were usually kept in specially made boxes, spoons would most often be stored in small, open wooden racks that hung on the wall. Here, they would be conveniently on hand to the cook, as well as acting as a decorative feature in the kitchen. Sometimes spoon racks were combined with knife boxes, while others might incorporate a compartment to hold scouring and cleaning materials. The racks themselves ranged from plain and simply made to beautifully carved and painted – perhaps the more elaborately decorated spoon racks were given as gifts in a similar manner to the love spoons.

Left - ON THE WALL OF THIS TYPICAL COUNTRY KITCHEN HANGS A COLLECTION OF WOODEN SPOONS HOUSED IN A SIMPLE, CUT-OUT WOODEN SPOON RACK. THIS HAS BEEN MADE RECENTLY AND GIVEN A TIME-WORN, ANTIQUE APPEARANCE BY DISTRESSING THE PAINTWORK.

Above - SPOONS WERE ONCE REGARDED WITH MORE RESPECT THAN THEY ARE TODAY, AND MUCH CARE AND ATTENTION WENT INTO THEIR MAKING. HIGHLY DECORATED SPOONS WERE GIVEN AS LOVE TOKENS AND WOULD OFTEN BE PROUDLY DISPLAYED IN A SPECIALLY MADE SPOON RACK.

SPOON RACK

ABILITY LEVEL: Novice/ Intermediate

SIZE: 13 x 9 x 5⅝in (330 x 229 x 143mm)

MATERIALS: Pine, Cherry

CUTTING LIST:
1 front
8 x 6 x ⅜in (203 x 152 x 10mm)

1 back
8 x 6 x ⅜in (203 x 152 x 10mm)

2 sides
9 x 5⅝ x ⅜in (229 x 143 x 10mm)

2 step fronts
8¾ x 1½ x ⅜in (222 x 38 x 10mm)

3 step tops
9 x 1⅞ x ⅜in (229 x 47 x 10mm)

See template patterns on page 151 for the back and front pieces.

SPOONS

ABILITY LEVEL: Novice/Intermediate

SIZE: 10 x 2½ x 1½in (254 x 64 x 38mm)

MATERIALS: Sycamore, Lime, Beech

CUTTING LIST:
10 x 2½ x 1½ in (254 x 64 x 38mm)

All measurements are given in inches, with the equivalents in millimetres indicated in brackets.

SPOON RACK METHOD:

1. Mark out the required pieces and cut them to the sizes given.

2. On each of the two side pieces, mark out the "step" shaping. Take care when measuring and marking out to ensure that the separate pieces fit at the assembly stage.

3. Cut each side piece out to the drawn shape. The sawn edges will later be covered, but it is a good idea to clean them up to encourage a good glued fit of the step fronts and tops.

4. Trace the full-sized template patterns of the back and front pieces (see page 151) and transfer these shapes to the appropriate pieces of wood.

5. Cut these pieces to shape (see page 137 for advice on cutting wood). Cut the internal shape with a coping saw after first drilling through the wood.

6. Clean off all marks and sand smooth.

7. Mark out the three step top pieces to accommodate the spoons as shown, or to any other configuration of holes and slots of your choice.

8. Drill or cut them as required. Drill through into a waste piece of wood to prevent the underside splintering. Sand back any rough edges.

9. Round over or bevel the front edges and ends of each step top.

10. Check that everything fits together correctly, and in particular, that the two step front pieces fit neatly under the overhang of the step tops.

11. Now clean off all surface marks and pencil lines before assembly.

12. Glue and nail the spoon rack together (see pages 140 and 141 for advice). Begin by assembling the front piece between the two side pieces and then add the back piece.

13. Next, put the two step fronts in position and, finally, add the three step tops, beginning at the bottom.

14. Wipe off any surplus glue, punch all nail heads below the surface and fill the indentations. Leave the piece to dry.

15. Clean up and apply a finish of your choice (see pages 146-7).

SPOONS METHOD:

1. Traditionally, wooden spoons were made by splitting a small sycamore log, about 4in (100mm) in diameter, into two halves and then roughly chopping the outside shape with a sharp, short-handled axe.

2. After this, the bowl was hollowed out using a special crooked or bent knife. The traditional Welsh carving tool (a *twca cam*) has a short, hooked blade and a straight handle some 18in (457mm) in length. Today, hooked knives, often of Swedish origin, are readily obtainable and can be used successfully instead.

3. Final shaping and finishing was accomplished by means of another small knife and a spokeshave.

4. Spoons can also be shaped by sawing and hollowing out using a curved woodcarver's gouge. The most suitable type is the long, bent gouge designed for scooping out concave shapes. A medium size, medium sweep gouge is best; a ¾in (19mm) No. 6 is fine for the job. You must keep the gouge sharp, however (see page 138 for advice).

5. In this method, the bowl is hollowed out first, before the outside is shaped. This allows the work piece to be held safely whilst the hollowing out takes place.

6. Select the material and mark out the shape of your spoon and then cramp the piece securely to a bench in a comfortable working position.

7. Start at the centre and work outward and, more or less concentrically, start to remove waste wood from the bowl. Use the gouge with a scooping action, going into and out of the material to remove a chip of wood each time. Don't dig in and take care not to go too deep. Aim to get a good finish from a sharp gouge whenever possible.

8. Remove the piece from the cramp and saw the outside to shape (see page 137 for advice).

9. Complete the shaping of the outside by whittling with a knife, or use a rasp and file. Finish off with glasspaper for a smooth appearance, if required. If shaped with a sharp knife, the tool marks can add character if they are left showing.

10. Don't apply any finish. After use, clean spoons by washing and occasional scouring. Never leave a wooden spoon soaking in water for any length of time.

11. Try making some of the alternatives shown in the opening photograph. Sometimes handles had simple, carved decoration, and this could be added if you wish.

SCOOPS &
LADLES

The name "scoop" derives from the old Dutch word *schope* and is also related to the Middle High German *scephan*, which means to ladle. While the words scoop and ladle are often used synonymously, scoops generally have short handles and are used for such dry goods as flour, pulses, and herbs, while ladles usually have long handles and are intended mainly for use with liquids.

Another distinction between the two is that scoops tend to be broader and flatter than ladles, but both – made of wood – were in common use in the households, and especially the kitchens, of countless generations of people before the introduction of plastics and stainless steel. There, they played an important part in both the preparation and serving of food and drink, often being used for mixing and measuring, along with spoons, as well as for transferring ingredients from one container to another or from one cooking vessel into another. They were also to be found in the farm dairy, for milk, and in butter and cheese making – a specially perforated scoop was used to skim the lighter cream from the whey.

It is not unusual to find ladles with spouts, like jugs, to help direct the flow of the liquid more accurately, and often they have hooked handles, too, so that they can be hung up out of the way or, conveniently, over the side of the container they are being used in. The ladle shown in the project is a short-handled ladle known as a churn ladle. Note the large hooked handle, which not only allows it to be hung up, but also forms a steady support when placed down, full of milk, on a flat surface. Along with other wooden utensils and implements, such ladles were in regular use in dairies well into the 20th century.

All types and designs of ladles and scoops were made, shaped and carved by local craftsmen or by members of the household. When it was available, sycamore would have been the preferred material to work with because it did not impart any smell or taste. Although primarily utilitarian, some were decorated with carvings, especially on their handles, while others would have been made from exotic imported woods. Ladles, or dippers, with quite small bowls – also known as punch or cordial ladles – were often quite intricately made. These ladles were kept especially for serving these beverages on formal occasions.

Wooden ladles and scoops are among the most collected of kitchen memorabilia, and their popularity is almost certainly attributable to the fact that so much in the way of kitchenware these days is either made from metal or plastic. Wooden utensils are so much more simple and utilitarian compared with many of their modern counterparts, and their well-used, well-worn appearance gives them considerable character and charm.

Above - AN 18TH-CENTURY DINING ROOM DRESSER PROVIDES THE IDEAL LOCATION TO DISPLAY A RANGE OF 18TH- AND 19TH-CENTURY KITCHENWARE. AMONG THEM ARE TWO WELL-USED WOODEN SCOOPS, A LONG-HANDLED LADLE AND TWO HIGHLY DECORATIVE WOODEN BUTTER MOULDS.

Right - WHETHER OLD OR NEW, WOODEN SPOONS AND SCOOPS — AND ALL MANNER OF OTHER DOMESTIC UTENSILS, TOO — SERVE BOTH A PRACTICAL AND A DECORATIVE PURPOSE IN TODAY'S KITCHEN. THEY ARE IMMENSELY SATISFYING TO HANDLE, AND SCOOPS IN PARTICULAR MAKE EXCELLENT SERVERS.

ABILITY LEVEL: Novice/Intermediate

SIZE: 12 x 6 x 3in (305 x 152 x 76mm)

MATERIALS: Sycamore, Beech, Lime

CUTTING LIST:
(**Flour scoop**) 10 x 5 x 2½in (254 x 127 x 64mm)

(**Churn ladle**) 10 x 6 x 4in (254 x 152 x 101mm)

(**Ladle with spout**) 13 x 5 x 3in (330 x 127 x 76mm)

All measurements are given in inches, with the equivalents in millimetres indicated in brackets.

METHOD:

Flour scoop (1in/25mm squares)

1. Working in the traditional way, a small, often unseasoned log would be selected. This would be split in two and a scoop or ladle chopped out and shaped from each half using a short-handled, very sharp axe.

2. The bowl's inner shape was then hollowed out using a variety of tools, including curved gouges, hooked knives or – for larger pieces of wood – a small hand adze. The bowl of the scoop or ladle would be completed with a rounded carving gouge or, in some areas (Wales in particular), with a special hooked knife. A curved woodcarver's gouge, of the type known as a long bent gouge, is suitable for this job. The final shaping and finishing of the outside was done with either a short-bladed knife or a drawknife or spokeshave.

3. Early makers were able to use these tools with great skill and little danger to themselves. However, the novice is strongly advised to employ safer methods of working, at least to begin with.

4. More modern methods of working include using sawn pieces of wood, which are marked out in outline and then partially hand or band sawn to the required outside shape. The inside shape of the bowl is produced by carving with the workpiece safely cramped to the bench.

5. To make the flour scoop, mark out the shape on the piece of wood by enlarging and using the pattern produced here. First, mark out and saw only to the plan shape. If you are hand sawing, make sure that the piece is held securely in a vice.

6. With the piece cramped by the handle portion, hollow out the concave scoop with a carving gouge. Begin at the front (open) end of the scoop and work gradually backwards in stages, biting deeper into the wood each time. Finish off using lighter, longer strokes with the gouge to leave the wood as smooth as you can.

7. When you are satisfied with the inside shape and surface, mark in the side view and

remove the waste wood down to the lines you have drawn (mainly under the handle). Sawing by hand is best and safest. Complete the outside shape with a spokeshave or use a rasp and file. Next, shape up the handle and bring the front to a firm edge.

8. Finish off the flour scoop by sanding the wood until it is smooth.

Churn ladle (1in/25mm squares)

1in (25)
diameter hole

9. Because of the generous shape of the churn ladle, you will need a substantial piece of wood. As before, mark out its plan and side views, but do not saw it to shape until after the bowl has been hollowed out.

Cramp the piece to the bench and, using a carver's gouge, begin at the centre and work outward, more or less concentrically, to

remove waste wood from the bowl. Use the gouge with a scooping action, in conjunction with a mallet if it helps you. Don't let the gouge dig in.

10. An alternative is to remove some of the waste wood by drilling it out. Finish off the shaping with a gouge or hooked knife.

11. When the bowl is satisfactory, saw to the drawn plan shape, then draw in the side view. Begin the outside shaping first by drilling through to form the inside of the hooked handle, as shown. Then hand saw the waste wood away to the drawn lines.

12. Using tools of your choice, shape the outside of the bowl and handle. Keep the hook of the handle fairly substantial so that it does not break across the end grain, and keep its lower edge flat so that it make a good support when the ladle is at rest. Finish off by sanding it smooth.

Ladle with spout (1in/25mm squares)

13. The ladle with the pouring spout has a shallower bowl and a long, round handle. Making this safely is best done by holding

the wood in a vice and working on the bowl first. More experienced woodworkers may prefer to work in the traditional way, whittling with a knife or gouge while holding the wood in the hand.

14. With the plan and side views drawn in, and the piece cramped to the bench, begin by hollowing out the bowl, as described for the churn ladle (see step 9). Take care in shaping the spout portion and leave it a little oversize at this stage.

15. When you are happy with the shape of the bowl, saw away the waste wood to the drawn plan and side views. Keep the handle full and square at this stage and start shaping the outside of the bowl. Pay particular attention to the shape of the spout to ensure that it pours properly.

16. Finally, form the round handle using a knife, spokeshave or rasp. Flare the handle out slightly where it joins the bowl to give it extra strength. Finish by sanding it smooth.

17. Like spoons and cutting boards (see pages 88 and 96), scoops and ladles may be left untreated and kept clean by washing and scrubbing them. Never leave them soaking in water for hours at a time.

18. Good work is characterized by good proportions and bowl edges that are strong but not too thick. Final shaping with sharp cutting tools gives a more pleasing texture than a too-smooth finish obtained by sanding.

CUTTING BOARDS

One of the most useful, and certainly one of the most often used, items in the kitchen has always been the traditional wooden cutting board. As well as having pride of place on the breakfast table when slicing bread and cheese, cutting boards are invaluable accessories in the preparation of all manner of vegetables, meat and fish. Cutting boards feature prominently not only in the kitchens of country-style cottages but also in large, up-to-the-minute modern domestic and commercial kitchens. Even in today's world of ready-prepared convenience foods and pre-sliced bread, they still retain their usefulness – and they look good, too.

As the companion to the good cook's most precious tool of the trade – a sharp, well-balanced knife – a cutting board makes an ideal surface for cutting, slicing and chopping, all of which, until the end of the 19th century, had to be done by hand. All manner of implements were made to complement the cutting boards of the day, not just knives, but also a range of cutting, slicing and chopping blades. Some of these were cast in one piece with iron handles; others had separate blades mounted on wooden handles. Curved blades were handy for chopping things like herbs and spices in round bowls and mortars. Cutting implements with straight or slightly curved blades were used with flat boards. Many of these had a handle at each end of the blade, to give a firm, steady grip, and some had multiple blades to help speed the work. The advantage of using a wooden surface is that it does not blunt the knife blade as quickly as some other materials, and, contrary to some modern ideas, if properly cleaned after use wood is not an unhygienic work surface.

Cutting boards are available in all shapes and sizes. Many are simply plain, rectangular boards, either made from a single piece of wood or pieces jointed together. Yet others have handles and a means by which they can be hung up when not in use. When kneading bread dough and for rolling out pastry (with a wooden rolling pin), especially large boards were used; often, these doubled as the lid to the wooden dough bin or trough. This held the prepared dough near the warmth of the fire to prove and rise before being baked. For slicing and serving bread or cake at the table, circular and sometimes decoratively carved boards were once, and still are, very popular.

The wood used for cutting boards, or any other wooden objects that come into contact with food, is important. It must be close grained and stable and it must not impart any taste or have any odour. It also needs to be clean-looking and able to be kept properly clean. Sycamore meets these criteria best, with beech and maple close contenders. Pine is often used because of its low cost. However, it is too soft and does not wear well with use. Ideally, a cutting board should be left untreated and should be cleaned after every use with a clean, damp cloth or brush. If the board has been used for preparing meat or fish, scrub it thoroughly with soap and hot water, rinse off and leave to dry. Traditionally, cutting boards were kept clean by scouring them regularly with wet sand.

Left - KITCHEN OBJECTS SUCH AS CUTTING BOARDS, IN ADDITION TO SERVING A PRACTICAL FUNCTION IN MANY CULINARY PROCESSES, ARE UNDENIABLY DECORATIVE. THEIR WELL-USED SIMPLICITY LENDS CHARACTER TO THE COTTAGE KITCHEN IN BOTH TOWN AND COUNTRY ALIKE.

Above - KITCHEN CUTTING BOARDS LEND THEMSELVES TO AN INFINITE VARIETY OF DESIGNS, FROM THE PLAIN AND PRACTICAL TO THE EQUALLY USEFUL BUT WHIMSICAL. IT IS POSSIBLE TO COME BY PAIRS OF ANIMAL-SHAPED CUTTING BOARDS, AND THEY ADD A RUSTIC TOUCH TO A COUNTRY-STYLE DRESSER.

ABILITY LEVEL: Novice/Intermediate

SIZE: 12 x 10 x 1in (305 x 254 x 25mm)

MATERIALS: Sycamore, Beech, Maple, Pine

CUTTING LIST:
A 12 x 10 x 1in (305 x 254 x 25mm)

B 14 x 8 x 1in (355 x 203 x 25mm)

C 10 x 10 x 1in (254 x 254 x 25mm)

See template patterns on pages 150-1 for handle of board B, and pattern on board C.

All measurements are given in inches, with the equivalents in millimetres indicated in brackets.

METHOD:

1. Select well-seasoned material wide enough across the grain to match, or at least approximate to, the dimensions given.

2. Where this is not possible, you can make boards up out of narrower pieces edge joined together (see page 141 for advice on edge joining). Make sure you use a good-quality waterproof adhesive.

3. Plane or sand both surfaces clean and perfectly flat.

4. Where required, draw the outline of the shape directly on to the wood and cut it to shape using any safe method (see page 137 for advice on cutting). Always cut on the outside (the waste side) of the drawn line.

5. The rectangular board (A) is easily marked out using a set square and ruler. The handle of the handled board (B) is marked out and cut to the pattern given on page 150. The circular board (C) is marked out by using a pair of compasses.

6. Clean up the sawn edge surfaces by planing any long straight edges, taking care with the end grain. Use a suitable file or other abrasive tool to clean up curved edges and to get into any awkward corners. Or use a spokeshave. Round over or chamfer the edges so that they are not sharp. Finish off with fine glasspaper.

7. The rectangular cutting board (A) is now complete (see also step 10 right).

8. The handled board (B) requires a ¼in (6mm) hole drilled through the handle to thread a cord for hanging.

5in (127) radius

9. The circular board (C) has one flat surface decorated with carving. To help you reproduce this design a pattern is given on page 151. You can trace this off and transfer it to your board or devise a pattern of your own design. Or you can leave the board plain and simply round its edges over.

10. For regular use, the boards should be left untreated with no surface finish at all. Keep them clean by regularly wiping them with a damp cloth and an occasional scrub in water. If a finished surface is required, apply several coats of vegetable oil to the wood.

Right - THE RUGGED APPEARANCE OF A WELL-USED BUTCHER'S CHOPPING BLOCK ON A COUNTER TOP AND THE SCRUBBED SURFACES OF THE CUTTING BOARDS DISPLAYED BELOW PROVIDE A STRONG CONTRAST OF TEXTURE WITH THE SMOOTH, POLISHED, DOUBLE BOW WINDSOR CHAIR IN THIS ENGLISH KITCHEN.

WALL-HUNG
CUPBOARD

Wall-mounted boxes for storing all manner of domestic odds and ends were once very common. As well as these, ranks of simple open shelving designed to help keep work surfaces clear of clutter, and for displaying ornaments and prized pieces of family crockery and similar family pieces, were supplemented in many homes by small cupboards of the type shown below. Cupboards such as these could be found in any room of the house. In the kitchen, one could be used for cooking utensils or for tinned or packaged foodstuffs and spices. In a bathroom, a cupboard much like this makes an ideal medical cabinet, while in a sitting or family room, wall cupboards could be used for housing books and important family papers and documents or as a liquor cabinet. If needs be, a lock could easily be fitted, especially if medicines or alcohol were to be kept inside. Cupboards used for storing food are often found with pierced fronts, or with front panels made of perforated tinplate, to allow fresh air to circulate inside to keep food fresh and the flies out. Early descriptive names for food cupboards include meat safe and pie safe.

The term wall cupboard obviously describes a container designed to be hung on a wall, and for this reason they are also often described as hanging cupboards. If they are further described as being enclosed then they also had a door – a seemingly unnecessary adjunct now, since in modern parlance many pieces of wooden furniture with doors can generally be described as cupboards. But this was not always so. Primarily, the cupboard or, more correctly, the "cup-board", or "cup-borde", was a medieval contrivance, which consisted of a supported board or plank of wood on which drinking vessels were placed during a meal. This use was to give rise to the parallel evolution of the sideboard and the dresser.

Another ancient name, now mainly used, and sometimes misused, by furniture historians and antique furniture dealers is, in fact, more closely related to the modern concept of the cupboard. This is the "aumbry" or "armoire", which is a box-like structure with shelves and, more important, a door. Early forms were made to fit into a niche cut into the fabric of the wall. By the late Middle Ages, however, freestanding versions had been developed. These were used for many different purposes, both secular and sacred. The livery cupboard, for example, had pierced doors for ventilation and was used to store the daily food rations for the servants and retainers of the great houses. From this came the term "liveried servant".

For the early settlers to Colonial America, an enclosed cupboard for the storage of food would have been a priority. The wall-hung cupboard described in the project that follows, although rather elaborate for a country piece, is based on one said to have been made in Pennsylvania in about 1750.

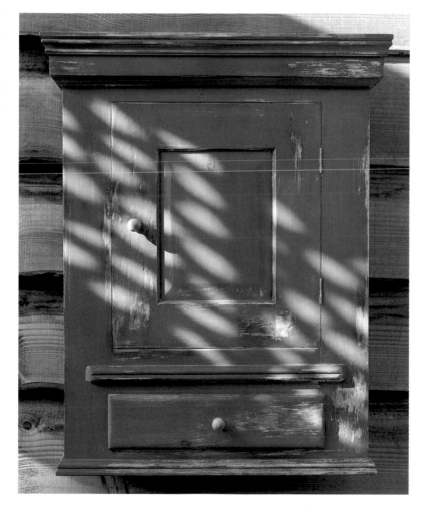

Left - THE GOOD COOK BELIEVES THAT THERE IS "A PLACE FOR EVERYTHING AND EVERYTHING IN ITS PLACE", AND THAT THERE CAN NEVER BE TOO MANY CUPBOARDS AND DRAWERS IN THE BUSY KITCHEN. THE SIMPLE DESIGN OF THIS WALL-HUNG CUPBOARD REVEALS ITS COUNTRY ROOTS.

Above - WITH ITS PAINTED, TIME-WORN APPEARANCE, THIS FINELY WORKED CUPBOARD WOULD FIND A PLACE IN ANY FARM OR COTTAGE KITCHEN DESPITE SUCH ELEGANT DETAILS AS THE CORNICED TOP MOULDING AND PANELLED DOOR – NOT FEATURES COMMON TO MANY TRUE COUNTRY-MADE CUPBOARDS.

ABILITY LEVEL: Experienced

SIZE: 27 x 20 x 9in
(686 x 508 x 229mm)

MATERIALS: Pine

CUTTING LIST:
CARCASS
2 sides
26 x 7 x ¾in (660 x 178 x 19mm)

1 top
18¼ x 7 x ¾in (457 x 178 x 19mm)

1 bottom
18¼ x 7 x ¾in (457 x 178 x 19mm)

1 mid shelf
18¼ x 6¾ x ¾in (457 x 171 x 19mm)

1 back
26 x 19 x ⅜in (660 x 483 x 10mm)

FACE FRAME (front)
2 stiles
26 x 3 x ¾in (660 x 76 x 19mm)

2 rails
16 x 3 x ¾in (406 x 76 x 19mm)

1 mid rail
16 x 3 x ¾in (406 x 76 x 19mm)

DOOR
2 stiles
15 x 3 x ¾in (381 x 76 x 19mm)

2 rails
10 x 3 x ¾in (254 x 76 x 19mm)

1 panel
10 x 8 x ½in (254 x 203 x 12mm)

DRAWER
1 front
13 x 3 x ½in (330 x 76 x 12mm)

2 sides
7 x 3 x ½in (178 x 76 x 12mm)

1 back
13 x 2½ x ½in (330 x 64 x 12mm)

1 onset front
13½ x 3½ x ½in (343 x 89 x 12mm)

1 bottom
12 x 7 x ¼in (305 x 178 x 6mm)

4 guides
7 x ½ x ½in (178 x 12 x 12mm)

2 supports
7 x 5½ x ½in (178 x 140 x 12mm)

CORNICE
1 top rail
21 x 3 x ¾in (533 x 76 x 19mm)

2 side rails
9 x 3 x ¾in (229 x 76 x 19mm)

moulding
approx 9ft of ¾ x ¾in (2743 x 19 x 19mm)

All measurements are given in inches, with the equivalents in millimetres indicated in brackets.

METHOD:

1. Select materials and cut all parts to size. Take care to cut all ends squarely and accurately (see page 137 for advice). Keep all related parts together – for example, drawer parts, carcass parts, etc.

2. Begin by planing and edge gluing the pieces needed to make wider boards, if necessary.

3. Construct the carcass first. Mark out and cut the through housings, ¼in (6mm) deep, in the side pieces to accommodate the top, mid

dle and bottom shelves. Cut a ⅜in (10mm) rebate for the back (see page 142 for advice on rebates).

4. Test fit, without using glue, to check that everything fits and is square. Disassemble and clean off any surface marks.

5. Apply glue and assemble the carcass. Again, check that it is square and hold it together with cramps until it is dry.

6. Make up the front face frame using mortises and tenons (see page 144 for advice on making these joints). Check the lengths of the components. The frame can be slightly larger than the carcass to allow for planing to a flush fit later.

7. Mark out and cut the mortises into each of the stiles, and mark and cut the tenons on each end of the rails. Since the stiles and rails are ¾in (19mm) thick, the mortises and tenons will be ¼in (6mm).

8. Check that each joint is a good fit. Then test fit, without glue, and check that the frame is square. Disassemble and clean off any surface marks.

9. Apply glue and make up the front face frame. Hold it with cramps and check that it has not twisted out of square.

10. The door is of frame and panel construction and has haunched mortise and tenon joints. This, too, should be slightly oversized so that it can be planed to a good fit within the door opening.

11. Cut a ¼in (6mm) wide, ¼in (6mm) deep groove along the inside edge of all four door frame pieces (see page 142) to accommodate the panel.

12. Mark out and cut the mortises into both stiles.

13. Mark out and cut the haunched tenons on each end of the rails. The haunch is trimmed to fit and fill the exposed ends of the grooves made in the stiles (see page 142 for grooving and for making joints).

14. Test fit each joint and then assemble the door frame, without using glue, to check that it is square.

15. While the door frame is assembled, measure the opening for the door panel. Add ⅜in (10mm) to both the length and the width (to fit into the frame groove). Now disassemble the frame.

16. Cut the door panel to the precise dimensions determined in step 15. Plane a long bevel all around the panel, as shown, and test fit it in the door frame groove.

17. Assemble the door frame and panel, without using glue, bevel facing outward. Check for square and then disassemble and clean off any surface marks.

18. Glue and assemble the door, but do not glue in the panel. Hold the frame together with cramps and check for square.

19. Attach the front face frame to the carcass by gluing and nailing. Punch the nail heads below the surface and fill the indentations. Plane off the frame overlap.

20. Try the door for size in the opening and then trim it to a tight fit. Mark the position of the hinges and chisel out the hinge housings. Test fit and hang the door.

21. To simplify the making of the drawer, through dovetail joints have been used (see page 143 for advice on joints). The onset, or lipped false front, conceals the joints at the

front and also eliminates the need for any drawer stops.

22. Begin by making the drawer front fit the opening. Cut the back to the same length as the front, and the side pieces the same width as the front. Check that the ends are square and mark adjoining parts.

23. Now mark out and cut the dovetail "tails" on the drawer side pieces (see page 143 for advice).

24. Mark out the dovetail "sockets" using the "tails" cut in step 23 as a template.

25. Cut the dovetail "sockets" (see page 143 for advice) and test fit each joint, but avoid handling them too often.

26. Assemble the drawer parts, without using glue, and check for square. Disassemble the drawer and clean off any surface marks ready for the next stage.

27. Apply glue and assemble the drawer. Cramp it together and check again for square. When dry, clean off surplus glue in the joint areas.

28. Fit the drawer bottom, with the grain running from side to side, on slips of wood at the sides and front. Pin it where it passes and overhangs the back. Do not use glue.

29. Glue and nail the onset false front into position, with an equal overhang all around. Punch the nail holes below the surface and fill the indentations with woodfiller or a mixture of glue and sawdust. When the glue is thoroughly dry, round over the overhanging front edges.

30. The drawer runs between supports and simple guides, fitted as shown.

31. Cut the cornice pieces to length and mitre their mating ends. On the lower edges of each piece, plane a ½in (12mm) bevel.

32. Test fit and then glue and nail the cornice into place.

33. Mitre and test fit the top and bottom mouldings. Glue and pin them into position when you are satisfied. Apply the centre moulding.

34. Cut the back to size and pin it into its rebate.

35. Make or buy matching knobs for the door and drawer. Drill tight holes for these and glue them into place.

36. The finish on the original cupboard is matt blue paint applied over layers of earlier paint. See pages 146-7 for ways of achieving a similar antique paint finish.

Right - WALL-HUNG CUPBOARDS COME IN ALL SHAPES AND SIZES AND VARY FROM THE MOST ELABORATE TO THOSE OF SIMPLE CONSTRUCTION. THIS LONG, NARROW CUPBOARD HAS A PLAIN BOARDED DOOR OF PAINTED PINE AND AN UNUSUAL ROOF-LIKE, ARCHED TOP.

Bedrooms & Bathrooms

BEDROOMS

There is little to match the comfortable intimacy of a country-style cottage bedroom. Old pine furniture – original or stripped and rewaxed or repainted in the cool, earth shades of the countryside – or the rich patina of polished oak, cherry, or beech, blend beautifully with coloured textiles and the sprig patterns of country bedroom wallpaper, bed linen and curtaining.

The bedroom as we think of it today, however, did not really exist until about the beginning of the 18th century. Cottage bedrooms (created in the free space beneath the eaves of the roof) were small and dark and furnished with little more than a bed and bedside chair. In the "big houses", while the family slept in quite large rooms, their servants slept in attic rooms, which were slightly more spacious than the cottage attic, and often had a dormer window as well to admit some light. These two factors, and a few extra bits of furniture, often discarded from other parts of the house, allowed for more creativity. Thus, much of the inspiration for today's image of the country bedroom comes not from the humble cottage but from the wealthier household, since more of these examples have survived.

BEDS

The bed – the focal point of any bedroom – can be a simple wooden bedstead, a bare box bed, or perhaps an old truckle or trundle bed. These beds had wheels and were originally kept tucked away under a larger bed in the bedrooms of the better-off, and they would be wheeled out when required for the use of a servant or a child. The so-called "sleigh" bed – a Scandinavian development of the box bed – injects a touch of the exotic into the country theme, while, by way of a contrast, the stark austerity and utilitarianism of the Adirondack-style "twig" bed gives a true rustic feel to the country cottage bedroom. Beds with headboards lend themselves to restrained decoration, such as carving, piercing, or stencilling. Your tastes might be for a more ornate style of bed, with lathe-turned posts built in the Pennsylvania style. Or you may prefer a simple four-poster.

No matter how plain, grand, or rustic your choice of bed, there is no need to compromise on comfort. Any style of country bed can, of course, be fitted with a modern mattress, appropriately concealed with traditional bedcovers, linen sheets, embroidered pillow cases, and perhaps a colourful, hand-crafted quilt.

Top Left - MADE IN MASSACHUSETTS AROUND 1820, THIS BED IS A FINE EXAMPLE OF THE COLONIAL FOUR-POSTER STYLE.

Below Left - A LATHE-TURNED AND RAIL BED, THREE-DRAWER CHEST AND HANGING SHELF MAKE UP THE THREE KEY ELEMENTS IN THIS COTTAGE BEDROOM.

Right - RESPLENDENT IN A 19-CENTURY QUILT, THE ADIRONDACK-STYLE TWIG BED GIVES THIS BEDROOM AN INVITING COUNTRY COMFORTABLENESS.

STORAGE

Furniture for storage is an important consideration in the bedroom. Shelves can serve both a decorative and a practical role, and the hanging shelves characteristic of the Shaker style suit these particular requirements well. The traditional chest or blanket box, which was once used to store everything from personal clothing to clean bed linen and other effects, is still a useful item for storing bedding. It makes a tremendous contribution to the country cottage look of a room, especially when placed at the foot of a bed. Pine is a popular choice for a blanket box, but you can use other woods, too, especially if it is to be finished with clear varnish to allow the wood grain to show through. Less-well-figured woods can be painted plain or decorated in the manner of the Pennsylvania dower chests.

Storage furniture in the country house is rarely restricted to use in any one room, and plain chests of drawers, as well as more elaborate pieces with shelves or closed cupboards fitted above, find a place in the bedroom as elsewhere. These "children of the chest" began life when a frame-and-panel construction allowed for a front-opening drawer to be fitted in the bottom of the chest. The obvious advantage of the drawer over the box soon led to the development of what we now know as the chest of drawers, in which the entire framework is filled with drawers. Further changes saw these chests of drawers become higher and contain even more drawers, and so the "tallboy" came into being. From there they evolved into a variety of styles. Those made in the country style are generally of solid construction or are framed and panelled in pine, oak, or cherry. Chests of drawers are usually named for the number of drawers they contain – three, four, and five being the most common numbers.

Purpose-built dressing tables, complete with pivoting mirrors, are a comparatively modern development in bedroom furniture, and most would be out of place in a country-style bedroom. Instead, consider a small table with a separate, freestanding mirror, or one fixed to a wall above it, as a more suitable option. As an alternative, a wooden washstand, typically with a marble top, and complete with a matching porcelain bowl and jug might be the perfect solution for a country-style bedroom.

Left - FURNITURE FROM WIDELY DIFFERENT CULTURES AND REGIONS OFTEN WORK WELL TOGETHER IN COUNTRY-STYLE INTERIORS. THE BLUE-PAINTED CUPBOARD FROM MEXICO PAIRED WITH A RED STOOL FROM JAMAICA BRING A SPLASH OF COLOUR TO THIS NEW ENGLAND BEDROOM.

Top Right - AN OLD CHEST OF DRAWERS ALSO SERVES AS A SURFACE FOR A DECORATIVE DISPLAY – SUCH INFORMAL STILL LIFES EPITOMIZE THE COUNTRY STYLE.

Below Right - TRUE TO THE COTTAGE BEDROOM OF OLD, A SMALL TABLE IS USED AS A FORM OF DRESSER INSTEAD OF A PURPOSE-BUILT MODEL.

WARDROBES

Clothes cupboards or wardrobes may first have been used in churches as places in which to hang rich vestments and other religious robes. It was not until the 19th century that they came into general use in the home. Before this time, the custom had been to keep clothes folded in chests of drawers rather than to have them hanging up. Where clothes were hung, it was usually in a curtained-off alcove or perhaps in a built-in closet. In medieval times, clothes were sometimes draped or hung from a form of pegboard, not dissimilar in style to the later Shaker pegboard, which was fixed to the wall, although clothes were generally stored away in large chests.

Freestanding wardrobes are often large items of furniture, and although you might be able to squeeze one into a small cottage bedroom, its proportions may prove overpowering. Because of this, it is probably better to leave the wardrobe outside on the landing, as was frequently done in the past. Wardrobes do come in all different sizes, however, so if you persevere you may find one of the right size for your bedroom.

North European and Scandinavian country wardrobes were often decoratively painted in rich earth colours, with hand-painted or stencilled motifs featuring flowers and foliage. Others were distinguished by heavy mouldings and boldly executed carving. Such peasant art, imported into America along with the new settlers, forms the basis for the development of modern regional styles.

Above & Right - THE WARDROBE ABOVE IS FROM FRANCE, AND NOW STANDS IN ALL ITS CARVED SPLENDOUR IN A CONNECTICUT HOME. THE EXAMPLE ON THE RIGHT IS LATE 18TH CENTURY, FROM SOUTHERN GERMANY. ITS RICHLY PAINTED MOTIFS ARE REMINISCENT OF PENNSYLVANIAN WORK OF THE SAME PERIOD.

CHILDREN'S BEDROOMS

Early inventories occasionally refer to items of children's furniture, such as cradles, chairs, baby walkers, and similar objects. Numerous 17th-century pieces especially made for use by children, including diminutive beds, have survived to the present day. More often than not, these items of furniture would have been used in shared rooms, since separate bedrooms for younger members of the family were rare until well into the 18th century.

The earliest separate accommodation was the nursery, where children, at least those of the well-to-do, were kept day and night in the care of nurses and nannies. Children were dressed like adults and, even at play, they were being prepared for adulthood – at a time when the horse was the principal means of transport, the wooden nursery rocking horse was not merely a toy. (Most toys in the past were made of wood, and some of these early wooden toys have become extremely collectable and are much sought-after today.) In a similar way, with few exceptions – such as the cradle – children's furniture was designed as scaled-down versions of adult pieces of the period. Even four-poster beds were made to children's sizes.

The purpose-made and permanent nursery furniture probably reached its peak of popularity in middle-class families during the late Victorian and Edwardian eras, just into the 20th century, when large families were the norm. By this time, however, a change in attitude in the way children were brought up was beginning to have an effect on the running of the nursery and on the provision and furnishings of rooms for young people in general.

Nowadays, the nursery is no longer a permanent arrangement. It is used mainly for sleeping purposes only during the first few years of the child's life, and it is considered to be a bedroom designed to change as the needs of the child change.

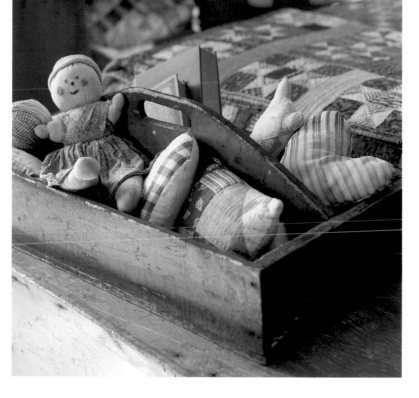

For the very young child, the cradle has withstood the test of time and remains popular today. In use for centuries, cradles have varied from the earliest woven type to the Gothic swinging cot. The more common type of rocking cradle, like the one described in the project on pages 121-3, has been in use since about the beginning of the 17th century. Examples were found in the cottages of the poorest workers as well as in the wealthiest of homes.

The earliest cradles were intended to accommodate the needs of babies up until about their third or fourth year. After this age, the child would graduate to a small-sized bed, or crib. 'Crib' was the name originally given to small beds with guarded sides – what we now rather confusingly call a cot. Known since Chippendale's time, in the mid 18th century, cribs had hinged sides, but now sides that slide up and down are preferred instead.

For the older child, the truckle or trundle beds already described (see page 106) are convenient and were frequently found in use in children's bedrooms, especially in rural areas. Where space was tight, built-in beds were also quite common, and these can incorporate valuable storage space beneath. Built rather like ships' bunks, these have developed into the modern, and very popular, two-tier bunk beds – a design that can solve the problem of making the best use of small-sized bedrooms.

Toy boxes or closets remain popular and are used by children for many years. They make convenient storage areas, too, allowing free space on the floor for play activity. Child-sized chairs and tables may also be needed for certain games and activities.

As an alternative to new or custom-made furniture, you may prefer to use second-hand pieces, repainted in clean, country colours, or given a protective coat of clear lacquer. But beware of splinters in well-used wooden furniture, especially if it is made from plywood.

Below Left - COSY AS A SHIP'S BUNK, THIS CHILD'S BED, LOCATED UNDER THE EAVES OF A FARMHOUSE IN SUFFOLK, ENGLAND, IS CONSTRUCTED IN PINE TO MATCH THE WALL AND SLOPING CEILING ABOVE. DRAWERS UNDER THE BED AND PEGS ABOVE TAKE CARE OF STORAGE MATTERS.

Above Left & Above - SIMPLE WOODEN TOYS ARE CHARMINGLY EVOCATIVE OF COUNTRY CHILDHOOD DAYS (*Left, Above*). THESE WELL-LOVED SPECIMENS HAVE CLEARLY GIVEN YEARS OF PLEASURE. THE UNUSED KNIFE BOX (*Above*) HAS TAKEN ON A NEW LEASE ON LIFE AS A PLACE TO KEEP A FEW HOMEMADE RAG DOLLS.

BATHROOMS

If the notion of a country-style bathroom conjures up thoughts of out-houses, cold floors, chipped enamel, and noisy, temperamental plumbing, don't despair. There are ways of combining 20th-century convenience with 19th-century charm. Although the bathroom is often one of the more neglected rooms of the house, it really is the place where you can give your creative instincts free reign. And if your bathroom has to accommodate such mundane things as, say, a water-storage tank, this can be built into an attractive wooden cabinet with extra shelves and storage space included.

THE USE OF WOOD

Unless your bathroom is a large room, it will probably contain very little in the way of furniture. Typically, you may find a wall cabinet, a few open shelves for storage, a stool, or perhaps a small chair. To introduce a flavour of country style, you could start by using wood for features such as wall panelling and accessories.

Wood panelling – either floor to ceiling or just halfway up – immediately injects a country-style atmosphere into a bathroom. Wood panelling was first used to cover rough stone and brick walls and, incidentally, it provides a reasonable degree of insulation, too, substantially reducing condensation levels.

It is common today for wood panelling to be extended to include the "boxing-in" of the bathtub itself. This modern innovation serves the additional function of concealing the plumbing – not usually the most attractive of bathroom features. Inexpensive tongue-and-groove boards made of pine can be used successfully for this job. All bathroom woodwork will be made more durable and easy to maintain if it is painted with, preferably, an oil-based paint or varnished in order to seal its surface.

Bare wooden floorboards, scrubbed clean or varnished for easy maintenance, can give your bathroom that ultimate country feel. And why not include a colourful rag rug for a better effect and more comfort. The addition of a nonslip backing will keep it safely in place even on the highest of gloss finishes. If there are children in the house, then more water may end up on the floor than in the tub. If so, then a cork mat, which is made from the bark of an oak tree, might be a more appropriate and durable type of floor covering.

ACCESSORIES AND FURNITURE

A wooden towel rail, the Victorian style of freestanding rail especially, always looks particularly fine in a country-style bathroom, while a wall-mounted mirror is generally considered to be an essential item. A mirror with a deep wooden frame can look extremely handsome. A large wall mirror, or, better still, more than one, may also create the impression that the room is larger than it in fact is.

If you have the luxury of a large bathroom, you also have the opportunity of introducing other items of wooden furniture. A small table or a chest of drawers, for example, could be a real asset. The table, with the addition of a wood-framed mirror, might serve as a dressing table, while the drawers will provide welcome storage for things such as towels and toiletries. And if there is still room, why not install a comfortable chair?

These items of furniture need not be new, in the best of condition, or even bought specifically for the bathroom. Unwanted pieces from other rooms in the house can be used. A coat of paint, perhaps using colours not used elsewhere in the home, will hide a multitude of past scratches, gouges, and rough handling.

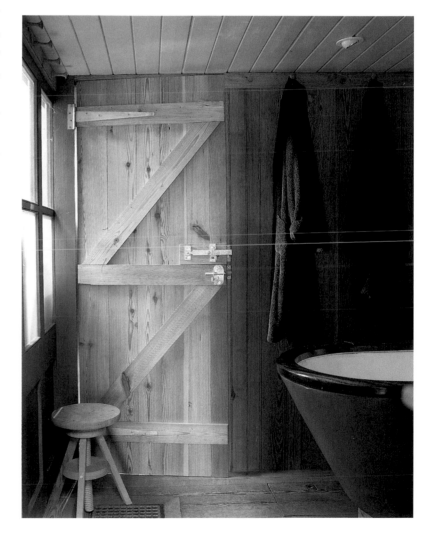

Left - HALF-HEIGHT PINE PANELLING PARTLY COVERS THE RAGSTONE WALLS OF THIS BATHROOM, FOUND IN A CONVERTED BARN IN RURAL KENT, ENGLAND. THE 19TH-CENTURY BATH ORIGINALLY HAD A SOLID WOODEN LID TO COVER IT WHEN IT WAS NOT IN USE.

Above - THE LEDGED AND BRACED DOOR IS MADE FROM PITCHED PINE RECLAIMED FROM INDUSTRIAL BUILDING DEMOLITION. IT CAME TO BRITAIN FROM THE UNITED STATES AS RETURN CARGO ON SHIPS DELIVERING MANUFAC-TURED GOODS DURING THE INDUSTRIAL REVOLUTION IN THE 19TH CENTURY.

SHAKER SHELVES & PEGBOARD

No book dealing with country woodworking techniques would be complete without a detailed look at the work of the American Shaker communities. This utopian religious movement – correctly but rather long-windedly known as The United Society of Believers in Christ's Second Appearance – originated in France but was led in the late 18th century by Ann Lee, the illiterate wife of a blacksmith from Manchester, England, who emigrated to the United States in 1774. Two years later, in 1776, she founded the parent Shaker community at Niskayuna, about seven miles from Albany, New York.

The Shakers, whose name derives from their agitated form of ritual dancing, are best known today for the excellence and simplicity of the work of their craftspeople. Part of the Shaker belief is that work is a form of religious devotion. Within their strict creed – "hands to work and hearts to God" – they created a simple beauty in all they did; functionalism predominated and ornamentation was regarded as unnecessary "worldly show". Their furniture was plain but always beautifully proportioned, and although it partly derived from influences from the outside world, these were restricted and refined into a style that is uniquely Shaker.

Of their many endeavours, the Shakers are perhaps best known for their fine furniture and wooden artefacts. Many of today's top furniture and interior designers have embraced the purity of Shaker form and style. At first, the Shakers' objective was self-sufficiency, but in due course what they made became much sought after by the "outside world", and before long they were producing not only what they needed themselves, but also a variety of items for sale.

The simple utility of the hanging set of shelves seen here is typical of their work. Shelves very much like these were made for use in all living and working areas of the house to hold personal effects, kitchen utensils and objects pertaining to work. As is evident from the photograph, their furniture is entirely functional, yet it combines practicality with a timeless elegance.

The manner in which the shelves are hung is a common Shaker practice. Rooms were routinely fitted with horizontal pegboards. These were often in continuous lengths and set at a uniform height, and so they constitute an important social and architectural element in Shaker interiors. Used to accommodate all manner of objects, pegboards, perhaps above all else, epitomize Shaker preoccupation with order and cleanliness. They provided not only permanent positions for such things as shelves, clothing, baskets, and so forth, but also essential temporary accommodation for such larger items of furniture as chairs to make floor cleaning easier and to create additional floor space when required in dual-purpose rooms that might, for example, see the kitchen instantly transformed into a meeting room.

Above - FUNCTIONALITY MARRIED TO AN UNCLUTTERED ELEGANCE ARE HALLMARKS OF THE SHAKER FURNITURE TRADITION. PEGBOARDS ARE THE IDEAL SOLUTION TO STORAGE PROBLEMS, WHETHER FOR HANGING SHELVES OR FOR CLEARING FREESTANDING OBJECTS SUCH AS CHAIRS OUT OF THE WAY.

Right - IN TYPICAL SHAKER FASHION, PEGBOARDS ARE USED FOR HANGING AND PUTTING AWAY ALL MANNER OF THINGS. THE ORIGINAL TURNED WOODEN PEGS HAD DISTINCTIVE SHAPES, WHICH VARIED ACCORDING TO THE SHAKER COMMUNITY OR VILLAGE THAT PRODUCED THEM.

SHELVES

ABILITY LEVEL: Novice

SIZE: 25 x 22 x 7in (635 x 559 x 178mm)

MATERIALS: Pine, Cherry, Beech

CUTTING LIST:
2 sides
22 x 7 x ⅝in (559 x 178 x 16mm)

3 shelves
25 x 7 x ⅝in (635 x 178 x 16mm)

PEGBOARD

ABILITY LEVEL: Novice

SIZE:
(**Pegs**) 5 x 1½ x 1½in (127 x 38 x 38mm)
(**Board**) 48 x 3½ x ¾in (1219 x 89 x 19mm)

MATERIALS:
(**Pegs**) Cherry, Oak, Maple, Beech
(**Board**) Pine

CUTTING LIST:
(**Pegs**) 3 pieces 5 x 1½ x 1½in (127 x 38 x 38mm)

(**Board**) 1 piece 48 x 3½ x ¾in (1219 x 89 x 19mm)

See template pattern on page 155 for side pieces.

All measurements are given in inches, with the equivalents in millimetres indicated in brackets.

SHELVES METHOD:

1. Begin by planing the edges of the shelves and gluing pieces to make wider boards if necessary (see page 141). Note that the shelves decrease in width towards the top: the middle shelf is approximately 6in (152mm) wide, while the top shelf is about 5in (127mm) wide.

2. Cut all pieces accurately to length, making sure that they are perfectly square across their ends.

3. Depending on the condition of the wood, plane or sand back all the surfaces so that they are smooth to the touch.

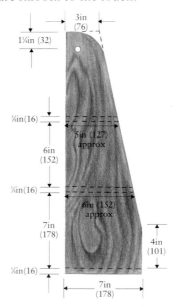

4. Cut both side pieces to the correct tapering shape as shown and plane or sand back the sawn edges.

5. Referring to the diagram, mark out the positions of the top and middle shelf housing and the rebate to accommodate the bottom shelf. Carefully check the exact thickness of the shelves before doing this, since all dimensions quoted when buying wood may be nominal only. Make the housing fractionally less than the shelf thickness to ensure a tight fit later on.

6. Cut the housings and rebate ¼in (6mm) deep and to the full width of the shelf (see page 142 for advice on cutting housings).

7. Check each shelf for fit. If necessary, shave wood from the underside of the shelves.

8. Drill a ¼in (6mm) hole, as shown, at the top of each side piece for the hanging cords. Before drilling, place a piece of scrap wood under the exit point of the bit to prevent the wood splintering.

9. Assemble the shelves, without using glue, to make sure that everything fits together properly. Disassemble.

10. Glue and assemble the shelves. If necessary, hold them together with cramps and check that all the angles are square. Wipe off any excess glue.

11. The bottom of the rebate joint should be further secured by careful nailing. Take care not to split the wood (see page 141 for advice on nailing). If the other joints fit tightly and are also nailed for security, cramping may not be necessary.

12. The shelves illustrated are made of pine and have been painted (see pages 146-7 for different finishing methods).

PEGBOARD METHOD:

1. Pegs would normally be turned on a lathe (dimensions are given). Simple shapes can be whittled by hand and finished off by filing and sanding. Alternatively, you can purchase ready-made pegs (see Directory of Suppliers pages 156-7).

2. If turning the pegs on a lathe, place each piece of wood in turn between the centres or fix each to a chuck and turn to the shape shown – or any other of your choice. Make sure that the tenon joint is true to size and is not too small.

3. If you are shaping the pegs by hand, make preliminary saw cuts all around as shown, and then cut or chisel into these to establish the rough shape of each peg before using files or rasps followed by abrasives to refine the shape.

4. Measure the size of the tenons needed in a test hole of the correct diameter made in a piece of scrap wood.

5. If using ready-made pegs, buy these first and check the diameter of the tenon joints before proceeding to the next stage.

6. Mark the positions of the pegs and drill 1in (25mm) holes (or holes of other sizes to suit) through the board. Drill into a piece of scrap wood to prevent the underside of the board splintering.

7. Try the pegs for size, without using glue.

8. Plane or sand the board smooth. It can be left plain or you can bead its edges using a simple beading tool.

9. As the diagram shows, a beading tool is easy to make out of a screw and a piece of scrap wood. When finished, round off the outer edge with a small plane.

10. Paint the board in your choice of colour; keep the paint out of the holes, however, as this will inhibit glue adhesion.

11. Treat the pegs with an oil or other clear finish, avoiding the joint area.

12. When the paint and other finish is dry, glue the pegs into position. When the glue is dry, saw off any protruding tenon joint at the back.

13. You can surface mount the pegboard by drilling and screwing it to an existing wall. Countersink the screw heads for a neat finish, and then fill in and paint over them. In a new wall, pegboards can be flush, recessed into the plasterwork.

HOODED
CRADLE

Cradles were once so commonly used that they transcended social boundaries and were to be found in the poorest as well as the wealthiest of homes. And because of their associations with infancy and childhood, and the custom of their successive use from one generation to the next, many have become cherished objects, even family heirlooms, irrespective of their origins or the quality of their design and construction. Sadly, the very earliest types of cradle have not survived the passage of time. These cradles were not made of wood but were woven – straw, rush, willow and any other pliable material have all been used successfully for cradle making – and, in fact, our word for cradle comes from the Old High German word *kratto*, which means "basket". The Gaelic name, *cliabhan*, literally means "little basket". The biblical basket that tradition has it carried the baby Moses downstream was, indeed, a cradle, and modern wickerwork cradles are still often called Moses baskets.

Some of the earliest examples of European wooden cradles were simple open boxes. These were made to swing between two uprights to keep the cradles suspended above damp and unhygienic floors. This type of swing cradle went out of use during the 16th and 17th centuries, but they appear to have made a comeback during the early Georgian period and later became highly fashionable.

In the intervening period, cradles mounted on rockers and placed on the floor came into common use, and this basic design has remained popular ever since. Some examples had panelled sides, like the chests of

the time, with rockers forming an integral part of the end panel or inserted into the lower end of the corner posts.

The tops of the corner posts often had turned knobs or finials, which proved useful as something to hang on to when rocking the baby to and fro, and, apparently, for winding wool. Some old cradles have small knobs running along the sides, and these were probably used to secure the covers in place. During the 17th century in particular, cradles were usually made of oak, but beech, elm, and various fruitwoods were sometimes used. They were frequently decorated either with carvings of stylized flowers or geometric motifs, often incorporating initials and a date. Decorative wood inlay was also popular, and holly and boxwood were often used to good effect for this woodworking technique.

Other cradles were more simple in concept and had solid-boarded sides and ends – the rockers in this case forming separate cross bearers and placed just a few inches in from the ends. In mild climates, where few bed clothes were required, cradles had shallow sides. In colder areas, cradles were made with deeper sides to cut down on draughts and provide room for more bedding. Many cradles of both designs had hoods. These provided both for extra protection from draughts and also, in the poorer households, from falling debris and drips from old thatched roofs. For easy access, the hood was often hinged so that it could fold back out of the way. The cradle described here is of the solid, boarded variety and has a simple hinged hood.

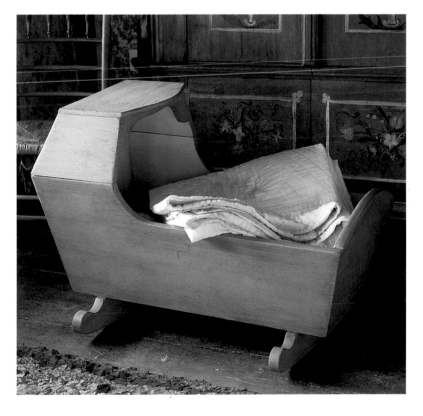

Left - Among the interesting collection of wooden furniture and woven artefacts found together in a Swedish mountain farmhouse is a crudely made, slab-sided rocking cradle of unusual design. It clearly reflects the traditions of a remote region.

Above - This solid-boarded variety of cradle has a simple hinged hood. It is based on an Irish farmhouse cradle dating from around the late 19th century. Despite being re-painted green, it still clearly shows the wear and tear of several generations of use.

METHOD:

1. Make the body of the cradle first. Use wide boards if possible or edge join narrow boards to make the required widths (see page 141).

2. Mark out and cut the side pieces as shown and clean up the sawn edges.

3. Mark out and cut the two end pieces and clean up the sawn edges.

4. The sides are joined to the ends using glue and either nails or screws. Screws are preferred. Nails should be 1½in (38mm) lost head or oval nails, knocked in dovetail fashion for extra security.

5. To use screws, drill and counter-bore the side pieces (see page 141).

6. Screw the sides and ends together without glue to check that they fit correctly, then disassemble for the next stage.

7. Then apply glue to the joint areas and join the sides and ends of the cradle. Wipe off surplus glue, check the cradle body is square and leave the glue to dry. Plug the screw holes and clean off flush or punch nails below the surface and fill.

8. Prepare the cradle bottom. Cut this oversize to the inside measurements across the bottom of the cradle initially. Then, fitting from the top, trim it to a bevel edge all around to obtain a wedge fit, flush with the bottom edges of the cradle body.

9. When this is achieved, glue and panel pin the bottom into position and leave it until the glue is dry.

ABILITY LEVEL: Intermediate

SIZE: 34 x 17 x 20in (864 x 432 x 508mm)

MATERIALS: Pine, Cherry, Oak

CUTTING LIST:
2 sides
34 x 14 x ¾in (864 x 356 x 19mm)

1 top end
17 x 14 x ¾in (432 x 356 x 19mm)

1 lower end
15½ x 12½ x ¾in (394 x 317 x 19mm)

1 bottom
27½ x 12½ x ½in (699 x 317 x 12mm)

2 hood sides
11 x 6 x ¾in (279 x 152 x 19mm)

1 hood back
17 x 6 x ¾in (432 x 152 x 19mm)

1 hood arch
17 x 4 x ¾in (432 x 101 x 19mm)

1 hood top
14 x 10 x ½in (356 x 254 x 12mm)

2 rockers
24 x 4 x 1in (610 x 101 x 25mm)

1 brace
27 x 2 x ¾in (686 x 51 x 19mm)

See template patterns on page 153 for cradle rocker and hood arch.

All measurements are given in inches, with the equivalents in millimetres indicated in brackets.

10. When dry, trim the joined edges of the cradle body flush and round over any sharp corners.

11. Plane the top edges of the cradle body level where the hood will fit.

12. Now make the hood. The dimensions in the cutting list are only a guide; use the actual measurements taken from your cradle, since they may differ slightly.

13. Mark out and cut the back piece first to establish the shape of the hood. From these same outside dimensions, mark out and cut the arch piece.

14. Cut the inside shape of the arch piece and round over its inside edge (see template pattern on page 153).

15. Mark out and cut the two side pieces.

16. Bevel the top and bottom edges of the back and side hood components to improve the contact with the cradle body and with the flat top, when it is fitted. Do this with a plane and don't worry if mating bevels are not perfect.

17. Holding them temporarily together, check that the hood back and sides fit and match up correctly on the cradle body. Adjust if necessary; take care not to make the hood components too small.

18. Glue and nail (or screw) the hood components together. Check that the shape of the hood still fits the cradle body and that it is square. Wipe off surplus glue and leave it to dry. Plug the screw holes and clean off flush or conceal nails.

19. Cut to size and fit the flat top. Glue and panel pins are sufficient, but avoid splitting the wood (see page 141).

20. Clean up the completed hood by planing joined edges flush and rounding over any sharp corners.

21. The hood is hinged to the cradle body (see page 102, step 20 for advice on hinges).

22. Now make and fit the rockers. Cut out the two rockers (see template on page 153) and clean up the sawn edges. Round over the rocking edges so that they don't become "carpet cutters". Cut out for the half lap joint with the centre brace (see page 143).

23. Cut the centre brace to size and shape and clean up the sawn edges. Cut out for the half lap joints with rockers.

24. Try the half lap joints for fit and adjust them if necessary.

25. Stand the cradle on the rockers/brace assembly and measure and mark its position on the inside of the cradle bottom.

26. Drill and countersink two holes along the line of each rocker and three holes along the line of the brace, as shown.

27. Fit the rockers and brace in position with screws through the bottom of the cradle.

28. Round over any remaining sharp edges and sand everything to a smooth finish. Apply a suitable stain, varnish or paint inside and out as required (see pages 146-7 for advice on finishing methods).

BLANKET BOX

The family chest, to which this chest is a kind of country cousin, is regarded by many as being the earliest form of furniture. Although primarily designed for storage, it once fulfilled an essential multipurpose role in the homes of our ancestors. In addition to holding clothing and bed linen and such valuables as documents and silver plate, they also served as seat, table and, sometimes, even as bed in what were the very sparsely furnished homes of the time. Furthermore, the chest was always packed and ready to travel and it could even be very quickly hidden away and kept safe in times of social and political unrest and upheaval.

The most primitive chests were of the "dug-out" variety, and were little more than hollowed-out tree trunks – hence the use, still common today, of the name "trunk" to mean a large piece of luggage or a travelling box. Thankfully, the modern descendants weigh far less than their predecessors did. As woodworking techniques improved and became more sophisticated, rough-hewn oak boards were joined at the corners with hand-wrought nails, and the case itself was heavily banded with iron straps, as much to stop the structure falling apart as for the security of its contents. Few chests of this type remain today; often they stood on damp stone floors, which eventually caused the wood to rot. The ironwork fared little better, since the combination of damp and the tannic acid released from the rotting oak corroded the metal.

During the 14th century, vertical end pieces known as stiles were added. These had grooves that held the ends of the now thinner, horizontal boards,

making an altogether stronger form of structure. When they were extended below the chest, these stiles became legs that raised the chest off the floor. During this period and later, chests became lighter in construction, with side plans an inch (2.5 cm) or less in thickness. Some chests were also made without stiles and instead had their ends joined by dovetailing.

The big leap forward in chest development came in the early 15th century with the introduction of frame and panel construction. Using this technique, mortised and tenoned frames have grooves in them so that panels are held in position without nails or glue, and are free to expand and contract without harming the structure as a whole. In due time, of course, the chest was to develop into the chest of drawers – but that is another story.

The boarded chest or box remained in use, however, particularly in rural areas. In time it, too, was improved upon, being made of seasoned wood and generally lighter in construction and with its ends united not be nailing but by a return to dovetail jointing. Its multi-purpose role also continued, for boxes of this type were used in all manner of ways – as tool boxes and boxes for books and blankets, as well as for the storage of personal belongings, animal feed and illicit alcohol. Their continued popularity was due in part to the fact that they were inexpensive to make, compared with a lavish chest of drawers, and partly to the fact that, where prepared wood was scarce and woodworking experience in short supply, they were economical in terms of both materials and skill.

Above - A SIMPLY AND SOLIDLY MADE TRUNK CONSTRUCTED FROM WIDE BOARDS OF PINE. STANDING AT THE FOOT OF A RUSTIC-STYLE BED, IT CONTINUES A LONG TRADITION OF PROVIDING USEFUL STORAGE FOR BEDDING. THE SIDES ARE STRONGLY JOINED TOGETHER BY INTERLOCKING DOVETAILS.

Right - BOXES OF ALL KINDS WERE IN FAR GREATER USE IN EARLIER TIMES, AND THIS COLLECTION SHOWS SOMETHING OF THE DIVERSITY OF THEIR DESIGN. MOST ARE PINE AND PAINTED; SOME, PERHAPS ORIGINALLY LEATHER-BOUND, ARE STUDDED WITH DECORATIVE BRASS NAILS.

ABILITY LEVEL: Intermediate/Experienced

SIZE: 40 x 18 x 19in (1016 x 457 x 483mm)

MATERIALS: Pine, Cedar

CUTTING LIST:

2 sides
40 x 17½ x ⅞in (1016 x 445 x 22mm)

2 ends
18 x 17½ x ⅞in (457 x 445 x 22mm)

1 top
42 x 18 x ⅞in (1067 x 457 x 22mm)

1 bottom
40 x 18 x ⅞in (1016 x 457 x 22mm)

4 end battens
18 x 2 x ⅞in (457 x 51 x 22mm)

3 long battens
40 x 2 x ⅞in (1016 x 51 x 22mm)

1 centre batten
17 x 3 x ⅞in (432 x 76 x 22mm)

Pair "T" hinges

Brass box lock with brass plate
4 x 4in (101 x 101mm)

All measurements are given in inches, with the equivalents in millimetres indicated in brackets.

METHOD:

1. Ideally, this project should be made, as the original was, from single wide boards. If you can't locate suitable boards, you will have to edge join narrower ones to make up the required widths (see page 141 for advice).

2. Cut the two long sides and two end pieces to the correct width and length and make sure the ends are square. Select the face sides and keep these facing outward. Leave the top and bottom pieces a little oversize at this stage; these will be trimmed to fit after the side and end pieces are assembled to make the main carcass.

3. Carefully mark out the "tails" of the dovetail joints on the end pieces (see page 143) using the measurements given. Note: top and bottom tails are the largest at 2in

(51mm); all the others are equal divisions of 1½ in(38mm). Cut out the "tails".

4. Using the "tails" as a template, mark out and cut the "pins" or sockets (see page 143).

5. Test fit the mating dovetails, but not too often, and adjust as necessary.

6. Prepare for assembly by cleaning off surface marks and guide lines from the sides and ends, inside and out. Have cramps ready to hand, but if the joints are tight fitting these may not be necessary.

7. Glue up the sides and ends to make the main carcass. Cramp up, if required, and check that the work is square. Wipe off surplus glue and leave it to dry.

8. Cut to the correct size two of the end battens and two of the long battens and fit them to the inside of the carcass, flush with the

bottom edge. Glue and screw, or nail, the battens into place.

9. Trim the bottom to fit the outside dimensions of the carcass. Secure it in place with countersunk screws, staggering them at about 4in (101mm) intervals on the ends, and at 8in (203mm) intervals along the sides.

10. This method of fitting the bottom is true to the original rather than being the best technique. A better method is to trim the bottom to fit inside the carcass so that it rests on the battens fitted on the inside.

11. Now cut the top to size. It should match the outside dimensions across the width of the carcass but overhang the two end battens

(when fitted) so that it does not interfere with the ends of the carcass when the lid is closed (see detail).

12. Cut the two end battens to size and fit them to the top, as shown, by gluing and screwing, or nailing. Clean up the sawn edges and smooth over the sharp corners.

13. Cut the centre batten (3in/76mm) to fit, without interference, the inside dimension across the width of the carcass. Fit this square across the inside surface of the top. Use glue and screws for the strength needed when the lock is fitted.

14. The original chest had long, cranked hinges to secure the top to the carcass. These are now difficult to obtain, but you can use modern "T" hinges instead. Modify these by carefully bending them, as shown, or use ordinary butt hinges instead (see page 102, step 20 for advice on fitting hinges).

15. Make sure that the top closes without straining the hinges. Some adjustment may be required.

16. Fix the remaining long batten to the back of the box – flush with the top edge – using glue and screws, or nails. Lightly chamfer the top edge of the batten away from the carcass before fitting and cut away some of the wood at the hinge positions. When fitted, this batten prevents the top swinging back too far when opened.

17. Follow the illustrations here for fitting a heavy-duty lock to the box. Locate its position and drill through for the key hole. Then, on the inside, chisel out a recess to accommodate the body of the lock. The catch plate, which is supplied with the lock, is attached to the underside of the top close to the centre batten.

18. After fitting the lock, a brass plate measuring 4 x 4in (101 x 101mm) with a suitable key hole can be screwed to the outside, to imitate the original lock plate.

19. When everything is complete, clean off all surface marks and smooth any rough edges, and then apply the finish of your choice. The original had a stained finish, details of which are on page 146. If you have used cedar, leave the inside untreated since the odour of the wood deters moths.

FOLK BED

While Egyptian pharaohs slept on elaborate feline-footed beds of inlaid ebony and ivory, and Roman emperors reclined on silk-covered couches, the beds of our more immediate ancestors were little more than rough pallets or straw-filled mattresses. During the Dark Ages in Europe, when one large room served for both living and sleeping, these beds were spread on the floor or laid on chests or benches. Some would have been placed in recesses built into the wall, a little like ships' berths. However, even after separate but shared sleeping chambers were introduced, for lesser members of the household the mattress was the only bed they had.

Wealthier families placed their mattresses on wooden boards raised off the ground, away from draughts and vermin, on bedsteads. Our modern word "bed" is, in fact, a contraction of "bedstead", meaning "the place of the bed". These bedstocks, as they were known, consisted of a framework of four rails joined to short corner posts that formed the legs. Later, these rails were drilled with holes through which cords or webbing could be threaded, across the width of the framework, to support the mattress.

From this period onward, beds developed in various ways, the best known being those that included the use of draperies around the bed, which later led on to what we now call the four-poster. These draperies served a practical purpose, providing both warmth and privacy for the rich and noble. Initially, bed curtains were hung directly from the ceiling or from a suspended framework known as a tester. Later the tester was supported on four corner posts, which, in due course, became incorporated into the bed frame itself. It was the development from the simple bedstock, of what became known in the 18th century as the stump bedstead – in which the turned or square legs of the wooden framework were extended at one end and filled in with a plain head board – however, that provided the basic design for so many other beds. The supporting wooden laths, which had replaced the corded or webbed base, had by this time given way to the use of spring metal and, by the middle of the 19th century, the iron and brass bedstead had become fashionable. Country makers, however, continued to make wooden bedsteads and today they remain as popular as ever.

Left - THIS SOLIDLY MADE, SUBSTANTIAL BED, WITH BOTH HEAD AND FOOT BOARDS, HAS A DISTINCTLY FOLK ART FEEL TO IT. IT IS MADE FROM NATURAL FINISHED PINE. THE TWO HEART-SHAPED CUT-OUTS ARE A TYPICAL DECORATIVE MOTIF OF THE TIROL REGION IN THE SWISS ALPS.

ABILITY LEVEL: Experienced

SIZE: 80 x 56 x 44in (2032 x 1422 x 1118mm)

MATERIALS: Pine

CUTTING LIST:
2 corner posts
44 x 3 x 3in (1118 x 76 x 76mm)

2 corner posts
34 x 3 x 3in (864 x 76 x 76mm)

1 head board
53 x 32 x ¾in (1346 x 813 x 19mm)

1 foot board
53 x 22 x ¾in (1346 x 559 x 19mm)

2 side rails
77 x 6 x 1½in (1955 x 152 x 38mm)

2 slat rails
75 x 2 x 1in (1905 x 51 x 25mm)

12 slats
52 x 3 x 1in (1320 x 76 x 25mm)

4 wooden balls
3in (76mm) dia

4 bolts
6in (152mm)

These dimension are designed for a 75 x 54in (1905 x 1372mm) mattress. It is best to measure the mattress to be used, however, before starting this project and adjust dimensions as necessary.

See template pattern on page 153 for heart motif.

All measurements are given in inches, with the equivalents in millimetres indicated in brackets.

Note: After cleaning off all surface marks, you can apply a clear polish, stain or paint (see pages 146-7 for different finishes).

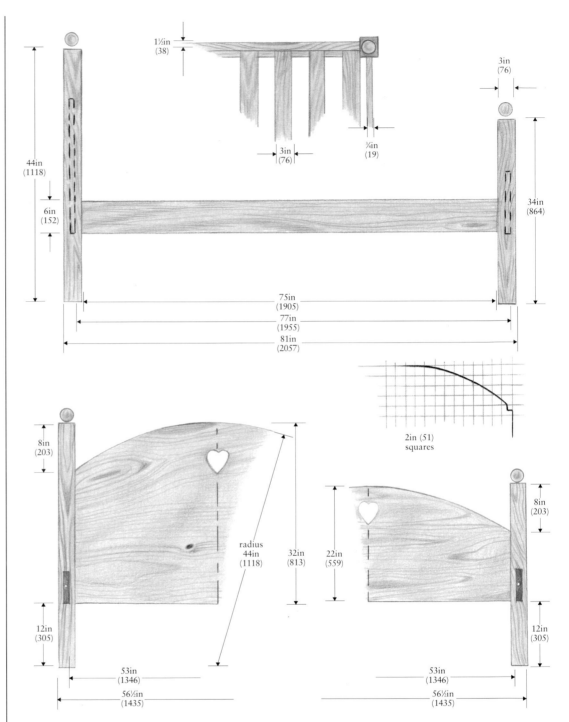

METHOD:

1. Begin by making up the head and foot boards by edge joining narrower pieces of wood (see page 141 for advice). Individual pieces should be as wide as possible so that there are not too many joints.

2. When gluing is complete and the work has dried, clean up the boards and check that they are flat. Cut them to the exact length and check that the ends are square.

3. Mark out and cut the curved top edge of each board. Round over the cut edges.

4. Mark out and cut the heart motifs. Use the template pattern on page 153.

5. Cut the corner posts to length and plane or sand the surfaces smooth. The ball finials are optional and may be fitted later. Make pencil marks on one end of the posts, as shown at the top of page 131, to avoid confusion later when marking out for jointing.

6. Head and foot boards are housed, at their full thickness, in mortises cut into the corner posts. Take measurements from the boards you have; these may differ from those given. Make the mortises a little undersized and trim the ends of the boards to a tight fit.

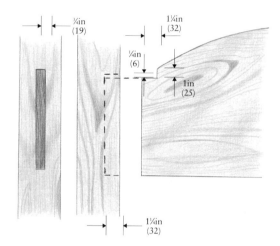

7. Each end board is notched at the top to fit the mortise and should be cut slightly short (see diagram). This is an allowance for any movement that may take place in the boards.

8. Test fit the end boards individually, without using glue, in their respective slots. Adjust if necessary by trimming the ends of the boards until the joints are tight and enter to their full depth. Disassemble and put the boards aside until later.

9. Mark out the correct adjacent face of each corner post for the mortises to accommodate the side rails. The pencil marks made on the end of the posts will help here. Cut these mortises (see page 144 for advice).

10. Cut the side rails to length and make sure that the ends are square. Plane or sand the rails smooth.

11. Mark out and cut the tenons on each end of the side rails (see page 144 for advice).

12. Test fit the side rail tenons and the corner post mortises, without using glue. Adjust as necessary for a good fit.

13. The head and foot boards are permanently glued into their corner post joints. The side rail tenons are not glued but held in their corner post mortises by bed bolts, as shown, to allow easy assembly and a useful knock-down facility. Bolts can be bought or made using threaded studding.

14. The diagrams show how to fit the bed bolts, but measurements may need to be altered to suit the bolts actually used. The nut recess is bored on the inside of the side rail. Place the post on its side on a bench,

with the rail tenon in place in its mortise, and bore the through hole carefully with a carpenter's twist bit.

15. Try each joint by fitting the bolt and nut and tightening up until the shoulders of the rail tenon come up tight against the corner post. Make identification marks on the rails and posts to aid reassembly. Disassemble ready for the next stage.

16. To fit the ball finials, if required, find the centre of the corner posts and bore a hole to house the fixing dowel. Glue in place.

17. Chamfer the long edges of each corner post and, if finials are not fitted, round over the top edges.

18. Now join the end boards to their respective corner posts. Place glue in the slot mortises, fit the end boards correctly and pull them in tight with cramps. Clean off any surplus glue. Leave to dry.

19. The mattress rests on slats, which are supported on rails glued and screwed to the inside of the side rails. Fix these rails so that the slats will be flush with, or slightly below, the top edge of the side rails.

20. Now assemble the bed frame. Make sure that the side rails fit into their correct mortises and that the bed bolts tighten up fully. Cut the slats to fit across the bed frame. Space them out evenly. Slats may be loosely strung together, nailed or stapled, to two lengths of woven tape. Screw the top and bottom slats down and the whole assembly will stay in place.

Tools & Techniques

TOOLS & TECHNIQUES

Most of the projects featured in this book require only the simplest of woodworking tools, so there is no need to have or buy an expensive or a complicated kit. Some basic knowledge of how to use these tools is assumed, however.

If you are a beginner, start with the projects which have been designed for the "novice" level and, by working through these, hopefully you will soon pick up the expertise required to undertake the more complicated "intermediate" and "experienced" projects.

All of the projects have been designed to be completed using hand tools only. Although immensely satisfying, working entirely with hand tools (as opposed to power tools) can be both tiring and time-consuming, as well as often requiring a high degree of skill. If, however, you have power tools available – and you know how to use them safely and competently – there is no reason why you should not press them into service. In my own work I often use a combination of methods: power tools for the initial, often repetitive, work such as sawing to size and planing to thickness; a combination of power and hand tools for shaping and jointing; and hand tools for finishing and detailing.

The original country woodworker would have had few tools at his disposal, and these would have most probably been general-purpose implements, rather than specialist ones, used for all manner of jobs around the cottage or farm. An axe and an adze would have been used for chopping and riving, for example; a saw and a few chisels for cutting; a drawknife, spokeshave, rasp, and files for shaping; a plane for smoothing; a brace and bit for drilling holes; a hammer and nails for fastening; and a knife for cutting and trimming.

Construction methods, too, would have been all-purpose and relatively simple, using whatever timber was available and most suitable for the job in hand. The fundamental techniques of woodworking – shaping and jointing – have been known for thousands of years, and working methods evolved from applications such as house and barn construction, fence building, wheelwrighting, and so on. The joints used were basic to all forms of woodworking: the mortise and tenon of the shipwright and barn framer is larger and perhaps cruder than that of the furniture maker, but it is the same joint; the foot-long trenels (tree nails) of the trestle builder are no different in principle to the smaller pegs used to secure the joints of a country-made chair.

The techniques employed in the projects section of this book would have been used as a matter of course by the early country woodworker, and while the methods of certain types of construction may not have been part of the daily routine, he would certainly have been familiar with them. However, the exact way and sequence in which the steps are carried out would no doubt have varied according to an individual woodworker's knowledge and level of skill. In the projects described, all of the methods given follow traditional principles that are accepted and in use today, but they are open to individual interpretation.

BASIC TOOLS

It is not easy to say what a basic set of tools is for a modern woodworker – much depends on what is to be made, on personal preferences, and what is affordable. But whatever you decide on, always buy the best quality you can afford, and then take good care of the tools that you have. Working with poorly made or misused tools is a handicap nobody needs.

The list that follows includes those tools which are required for the projects and it concentrates mainly on hand tools, together with a few of the most helpful and time-saving power tools.

BASIC HAND TOOLS

Tape measure
Rule
Marking knife
Carpenter's or combination square
Sliding T-bevel
HB pencils
Marking or mortise gauge

Crosscut or combination saw
Coping saw and blades
Small back saw

Smoothing plane No. 4
Spokeshave
Wood chisels
Block plane
Cabinet scraper
Curved carving gouge

Mallet
Pincers
Screwdrivers
Cross pein hammer
Nail punch

Wheelbrace or drill
Twist drills/Forstner bits
Bradawl

Rasp, half round
File, half round

Cramps

Sharpening stones

OPTIONAL POWER TOOLS

Electric drill
Orbital sander
Jig saw or band saw
Power router

DRAWINGS AND PATTERNS

Before undertaking any project in wood, it is helpful to have a drawing or plan showing the general shape and main dimensions of the piece together, preferably, with more detailed drawings of specific parts. There are two main ways in which drawings such as these may be presented.

The first is known as an orthographic presentation, which normally shows three views – front and end views, plus a top, or plan, view.

The second form of presentation is a perspective drawing, which may also be in the form of an "exploded" view.

Sometimes it is helpful to show detailed parts of a project, such as curves, as a pattern or template. Where these cannot be shown full size, they are drawn on a scale grid. Each small square of the grid represents 1in(25mm) or 2in (51mm), as indicated, and from this you can lay out a full-sized pattern using grid squares of the correct size.

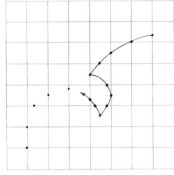

Squares = ½in (12mm)

WORKBENCH AND VICE

On the practical side, a space in which to work and a sturdy table or bench are your first requirements. This bench or table should also have some reliable method of holding wood securely while you are working on it. This usually means fitting a vice of some type, but you can also use other devices, such as bench stops or dogs and G cramps of various sizes.

A cast-iron carpenter's vice with wooden jaw facings is ideal. If, however, you have an engineer's vice, you will need to cover its iron jaws to prevent them biting into and damaging the wood. For light work, you can temporarily clamp a vice to the edge of your bench.

Another useful device is a bench-hook, which you can easily make up yourself. It can be gripped in a vice or held against the edge of your bench to provide a useful holding stop for work being chiselled or sawn, as well as helping to prevent damage to the bench top during these operations.

MEASURING AND MARKING OUT

Before you start making up any piece, you need to check that the wood is the right size and that it is straight and square and not warped. If you buy wood "ready planed" or "prepared" it should be fine to work with, but its machine-planed surface will require hand planing or sanding. Identify the best wide surface and an edge, plane them square if necessary, and then mark them with face-side and face-edge marks. From then on, all marking out and gauging should be done on or from these surfaces.

When you need to cut a board to length, make certain to check that the starting end is sound (not damaged or split) as well as square. If necessary, mark off a "waste" piece from the suspect end, measuring the length of the board from that mark. For a small board you can use a ruler, but a retractable steel tape is quicker when measuring a long board.

When drawing the line to indicate the length of board you want, mark it accurately and squarely by using a try square or an all-metal combination square. For precise work, make an allowance for the width of the saw cut, or kerf. Always saw on the waste side of the line, and if you want to cut several pieces from the same board, allow a generous ⅛in (3mm) waste strip for the kerf between each piece.

A well-sharpened HB-grade pencil is suitable for most of the marking out you will encounter. But for really accurate results the point of a sharp knife has many advantages, especially when marking wood across the grain. The knife point severs the surface fibres of the wood and leaves a clean edge after cutting. A traditional carpenter's marking knife has a thick, bevelled skew blade for this purpose – usually ground for right-hand users only. A small, lock-blade pocket knife is also recommended.

To mark lines parallel to an edge, you should be using a marking gauge, which is mainly used to gauge wood to both width and thickness prior to hand planing. Adjust it to give the mark you need by setting the required distance between the movable head and the pointed spur. To mark a line, press the head firmly against the edge of the work and push or pull the gauge away from you. Use a light stroke to reduce the danger of the point digging in and following the grain.

For less precise work, hold a pencil and your fingers as shown – this "trick of the trade" is known as finger gauging.

There are two other types of gauge you should be familiar with: the cutting gauge and the mortise gauge. The cutting gauge has a small blade instead of the marking gauge's spur, and it is most effective when marking across the grain. The mortise gauge, as its name suggests, is mainly used for marking out mortise and tenon joints. It has two pointed spurs – the inner one is adjustable so that you can mark out parallel lines of different distances from each other.

Compasses and dividers are most often used to mark circles or arcs, and you can use dividers to transfer measurements and to "step-off" equal divisions along a line.

SAWS AND SAWING

There are several different types of hand saw, some designed for general use and others for more specialized applications. The shape and size of the saw blade, and the number and configuration of its teeth, are what distinguish one type from another.

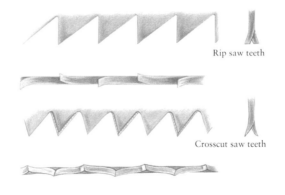

Rip saw teeth

Crosscut saw teeth

Rip saws, for example, are large, have between four and six teeth every 1in (25mm), and are used for cutting (ripping) with the grain. The shorter crosscut saw has between 7 and 12 teeth every 1in (25mm). Both types are used mainly in the initial preparation of timber and for cutting boards to size.

The tenon saw is the best-known example of what are called back saws. These saws have thin blades stiffened and weighted by a folded metal strip, usually brass, along their back edges, and they are used for accurate bench work and for cutting joints. Back saws are available in different sizes and can have from 12 to more than 20 teeth every 1in (25mm). The smallest type of back saw with the greatest number of teeth and finest cut is

generally known as a dovetail saw. Saws for cutting curved shapes use a narrow, flexible blade that easily breaks. In some saws, this problem is overcome by holding the blade under tension in a frame. The earliest type, known as a bow saw, has a blade held in a wooden frame tensioned by means of a twisted cord. More modern designs rely on a spring-steel frame and one of these, the coping saw, uses disposable blades that fit into pins tensioned by twisting the handle of the saw. You can fit the blade so that it cuts either on the pull stroke or on the push stroke. To make an internal cut through a piece of wood, first drill a small hole through the work, pass the blade through, and then fit it into the saw frame. The coping saw is used to remove waste wood from a dovetail joint (see page 143).

If you always make sure your saw is sharp, then sawing by hand should not be too difficult. Never force the saw into the wood. This is hard work and it tends to cause the blade to twist and jam in the kerf. For trouble-free sawing, support or hold your work securely, work with firm, even, fluid strokes, and use the whole length of the blade to cut with. Begin carefully – with a tenon saw pull back on the first strokes to establish a start – and work to the waste side of the line.

All of these sawing operations can be carried out with power tools, either portable or fixed. You can use a circular saw for straight cuts, while for straight and curved cuts you have a choice of the versatile jig saw, saber saw, a machine fret saw, or a band saw.

PLANES AND PLANING

The type of plane generally known as a bench plane is used to reduce the thickness or width of a piece of wood to the size required and to straighten or smooth a surface. Other types of specialist plane are used for grooving, moulding, and shaping; some of these may be multipurpose planes.

There are various types and sizes of bench plane, but they are all constructed in much the same way. Early planes had wooden bodies, or stocks, fitted with a blade, or cutting iron, held in place with a wooden wedge. The all-metal plane appeared in the middle of the 19th century and, due to the fact that it could be more easily and precisely adjusted, it became the preferred tool – although wooden planes are still in use today.

The metal jack plane is a "jack-of-all-trades". Its main use is to bring timber down to size, but, if it is fitted with a suitably ground and sharpened blade (see page 140), you can also use it for general straightening and smoothing. The length of a jack plane varies between 14 and 18in (355 and 457mm), making it particularly useful for planing long edges for jointing purposes. The metal smoothing plane is made in the same way as the jack plane, but it is shorter in length – 8 to 10in (203 to 254mm). It, too, can be used as a general-purpose plane, but it is intended mainly for finishing a surface after a jack plane or a machine plane has been used. Light planing with a sharp and fine-set smoothing plane can produce an excellent surface finish.

When planing a piece of work, make sure that the wood is securely and safely held in place. When edge planing, grip the work in a bench vice; for surface planing, either cramp the wood to the bench top or hold it between pairs of bench dogs. In order to achieve a smooth finish you have to plane with the grain of the wood, and not against it. On the end grain, plane halfway from each side to avoid splitting out the far edge. The lower cutting angle of the smaller block plane is best for end grain work.

As a general rule, when any plane is not in use, place it on its side on the bench in order to prevent damage to the blade.

For a particularly fine finish, especially on hardwoods, a cabinet scraper is the ideal tool. This device consists simply of a thin piece of good-quality steel, the edge of which is especially shaped and sharpened to

remove a delicate shaving of wood – like a butterfly's wing – when held and flexed between the fingers and thumbs of both hands and pushed forward over the wood at a suitable angle.

Although a spokeshave is not really a plane, it cuts in a similar way. Older, wooden-stocked spokeshaves have forged, tanged blades, which may be more difficult to adjust than a modern spokeshave but produce an excellent finish. Modern, metal spokeshaves are available in either flat or half-round versions. Used with a pushing action, a spokeshave makes chamfers and smooths narrow curved edges. A drawknife, which is used mainly for roughing-out work and for rounding and shaping, is drawn toward you with a firm pulling action. Drawknives are best suited to working on green (unseasoned) wood.

The specialist planes used for such tasks as grooving have become, more or less, obsolete due to the portable electric router, which does the same work with greater speed. Many of these hand planes are still available, however, and can be used.

Electric planers can be either portable or fixed. Hand-held electrical planers are not recommended and fixed machines can be expensive. Wherever possible, it is best to buy-in wood that is "ready planed" or "prepared" to size. If wood is machine planed, it will need to be finished off with a hand plane, or sanded, in order to remove the rippled surface left by the rotary cutting action produced by all power planers.

CHISELS AND GOUGES
Chisels for woodworking are of several different types and come in many different

sizes, depending on the work they are to perform: firmer, bevel-edged, paring, and mortise are just some of the names given to them. "Chisels" with a curved cutting edge should more correctly be called gouges. In addition, there are chisels and gouges made specifically for lathe work and for wood carving. Chisels are categorized by size – for example, the width of the cutting edge – and gouges by size and "sweep" – the degree of curvature of the cutting edge.

For general woodworking, the bevel-edge chisel has some clear advantages over the others, since its shape makes it particularly suitable for reaching into tight corners, cleaning out joints, and so on. You can, if necessary, strike the top of its handle lightly with a wooden mallet to get extra force behind its cutting action. Keep your chisels sharp at all times – it is easier to have an accident when forcing a blunt chisel to cut than when guiding a sharp chisel into the wood. And never hold your piece of work with one hand while using a chisel with the other – secure the wood in place and keep both hands behind the chisel's cutting edge. Make your first cuts across the grain of the wood to sever the fibres and try to cut with the grain at all other times.

SHAPING AND SMOOTHING
Although a cutting tool produces a better surface finish and is satisfying to use, there are times when you need to use other implements for shaping and smoothing. Rasps and files are abrading tools made from hardened steel. Rasps have coarse, triangular-shaped teeth and, because they remove wood quite quickly, they are used for rough shaping.

Files, which come in a variety of "cuts" from coarse to fine, are used more for smoothing. All can be readily bought in flat and half-round shapes – some files in round, or "rat's tail", section.

Modern abrading tools usually have tungsten-carbide grit welded to both rigid and flexible substrates, while another design incorporates a disposable blade of thin, hardened steel perforated with many sharp-edged holes. These holes form multiple cutting edges, but they leave a rough surface that requires smoothing.

For many shaping operations, you can use electric belt, disc, and drum sanders, while orbital sanders are often recommended for surface finishing. These devices can save you a lot of time, especially in production work, but they do not always leave a satisfactory finish. They also produce a lot of fine dust. Either the tool should have its own dust bag or you will need to wear a dust-protection mask or respirator.

Drills and drilling

Traditionally, wood-boring bits or auger bits fixed into a brace of wood and metal were used for drilling holes in wood. These were replaced by all-metal braces using interchangeable bits, or drills, together with another form of hand drill known as the wheelbrace. Metal braces, some with a ratchet action, and wheelbraces are still in use today, but the portable electric hand drill is the most popular and commonly used device when drilling holes in wood. You can buy a vertical stand to convert an ordinary electric hand drill into a simple but effective bench drill, while the multispeed drilling machine, available in both bench and floor-

standing models, is more suited to heavy and repetitive types of work.

Whatever type of drill you decide to use, there is a wide range of drill bits from which to choose. For general drilling, up to about ½in (12mm) diameter, ordinary twist bits, or engineer's drills, are suitable (A). An improvement on this design is the modified twist bit known as the dowel bit, or brad point bit (B). For more accurate drilling and for large-diameter holes, the saw-tooth Forstner bit is recommended (C), but this type of drill bit requires a power drill. If you are using a brace, the old type of centre bits (D) and auger bits (E) are probably best. For countersinking after drilling, use a rose-head countersink (F).

Hammers, screwdrivers, etc.

For the projects described in this book, a medium-weight cross pein hammer is most generally suitable. Hold small nails and panel pins between your fingers and start off using the tapered pein before switching to the face of the hammer to drive them home. A pair of pincers is useful for removing nails that bend or break. A wooden mallet is used mainly when you are working with a chisel or gouge, but you may also find it useful at the assembly stage of some jobs. Choose a medium-sized mallet with a head made from seasoned beech.

Screwdrivers are available in a wide range of sizes and types, with handles in different shapes and made from a variety of materials. What matters most is the size and shape of the end, or tip, in relation to the size and type of screw you are using. The oldest, and perhaps the most common type of screwdriver is the flat-tip blade made to fit

the traditional slotted screw heads; more modern types include various patterns of cross-head screws and screwdrivers. A flat-tip blade should fit snugly into the screw slot. Make sure that it is neither too large nor too small or you may damage the screw.

For starting screws, and sometimes nails, in softwood you may find a bradawl useful. A bradawl makes a guide hole and reduces the danger of the wood splitting. Start a screwdriver-tipped bradawl across the grain of the wood. When nailing or screwing into hardwood, and sometimes into softwood, it is best to drill clearance and pilot holes (see page 141). You can use a pin punch or nail set to sink nail heads below the surface of your work.

Cramps

You will find that cramps are useful items for holding work securely in place temporarily or for applying pressure to pieces of wood while glue dries and bonds them together. The most common kind of cramp is the G cramp, and there are several types and sizes from which to choose. The size is usually quoted as the maximum distance between the jaws of the cramp, and this may range

from 2in (51mm) to 12in (305mm). For holding larger or wider pieces of work, usually during the assembly stages, you should use sash or bar cramps. These consist of a steel bar drilled through at intervals to hold a pin that retains a sliding jaw or shoe. At the opposite end there is an adjustable jaw that takes up the final pressure. Always use cramps with protective blocks of wood to prevent the surface of your work from becoming damaged. There are numerous modern variations of both these standard types of cramps, some better than others.

ABRASIVES AND ADHESIVES

The words "sandpaper" and "sanding" are still frequently used as general terms for abrasive sheet materials and their use. Sand, however, is no longer to be found on abrasive sheets. Instead, materials such as powdered glass, crushed garnet, aluminum oxide, or silica carbide are used. These are deposited as grits on to various backings – cloth or paper – and in different densities and grit sizes. Sheets are normally classified by the type and grade of abrasive and by a number system related to grit size – the higher the number, the finer the abrasive. For hand sanding, many people prefer the pink-coloured garnet paper in grades 100, 150, and 220. Always sand with, not across, the grain of the wood, and wrap the paper around a sanding block to help keep the surface of the wood flat. Even if you use a power sander, you will still probably have to finish off by hand sanding.

The term "gluing-up" may in fact mean using any one of numerous adhesives that are now available. Traditionally, animal glue was used – it was all there was – and this had to be melted and applied hot. Today, there are upward of a dozen different types of adhesive, some intended for specialist applications. Those types based on PVA (polyvinyl acetate) are good, general-purpose glues, available for both indoor and outdoor use. Where a high level of water resistance is required, be sure to use a synthetic resin adhesive.

SHARPENING TOOLS

Sharp tools are a prerequisite for producing good-quality work – a dull cutting edge makes work difficult and is potentially dangerous. More cut hands result from pushing too hard with a blunt chisel than from working with one with a well-sharpened blade.

Sharpening takes in both grinding and honing. Grinding is carried out on a revolving grindstone, which usually leaves a coarse finish unsuitable as a cutting edge. After grinding, tools then have to be honed, or whetted, usually on a sharpening stone – either an oil-stone or a water-stone – to produce a sharp cutting edge. In normal use, tools can be honed several times before regrinding becomes necessary.

Many grindstones are electrically driven and most have narrow abrasive wheels revolving at about 3,000rpm (revolutions per minute) and are used dry. The danger here is that the steel being sharpened may overheat, and become soft as a result. The only way to avoid this happening is to dip the metal constantly in water to cool it. Machines with wider wheels revolving at only about 150-200rpm are more suitable.

Sharpening stones, usually oil-stones, come in three grades – coarse, medium, and fine – with the medium and fine grades being the most generally useful. Both natural and artificial stones are available. You should protect all types of oil-stone in a wooden box when they are not in use, and make sure that the surface is always lubricated with thin oil. The oil reduces the friction and floats off the fine metal residue produced by the sharpening process, which would otherwise clog the pores of the stone, causing the surface to glaze and become ineffective. Some stones use water as a lubricant. These stones are rather soft and easily damaged, but they do produce a fine edge. For really good results, the surface of your sharpening stone must be perfectly flat, so remember always to use the full width of the stone when sharpening tools.

When you buy new edge-cutting tools, such as planes and chisels, the blades supplied are ground but not honed. In order to hone a blade at the correct angle, hold it in both hands and place the ground bevel (which is about 25°) flat on the surface of the stone. Then raise your hands slightly to give an angle of about 30°, which is about right. Using moderate pressure, rub the blade back and forth along the full length of the stone's surface. This produces a fine burr, or wire edge, on the back of the blade (you can easily feel it with your thumb). Turn the blade over and, keeping it absolutely flat on the stone, rub the burr away to produce a sharp cutting edge. Check your results by holding the blade, edge up, to the light. Any bluntness will reflect light and show as a white line. For a superior cutting edge, strop the blade on a piece of leather dressed with oil and a mild abrasive.

One of the problems many beginners experience when honing, is rocking the tool or blade. This rounds the bevel over and stops it cutting properly. Maintaining the blade at the correct angle to the stone throughout the process can also cause problems. Gripping the blade firmly and keeping your wrists stiff help to combat the first problem, while a useful aid for both is the honing guide. This device runs on rollers and holds the blade firmly at precisely the correct honing angle to the stone while you push it back and forth.

WORKING METHODS

Joining wood

There are numerous ways of joining pieces of wood together. Some involve metal fastenings, such as nails or screws, or use wooden dowels, while some rely entirely on the adhesion of glued surfaces or a combination of these methods. In others, the wooden components themselves are shaped into interlocking joints, such as mortise and tenons, dovetails, and so on, which form, when glued, permanent constructions.

These jointing techniques have evolved slowly over centuries and few of them can be improved on. In recent times, however, the increased use of man-made composite materials – plywood, chipboard, and MDF (medium-density fibreboard), for example – and the requirements of ease and speed of manufacture and assembly have resulted in the introduction of other methods of fastening and joining, such as the so-called knock-down fittings and other instant-jointing systems. In this book, however, the emphasis is on the use of solid, seasoned wood and the traditional methods of jointing, and only those techniques required to make the projects will be included.

Using nails Nails are available in a wide range of types and sizes. The selection illustrated here includes those required in the projects. Nails are made of a variety of materials, including steel, galvanized steel, brass, copper, and aluminium and are known generally as wire nails or common nails, round and oval, and panel pins. Steel nails are suitable for most jobs – oval types reduce the risk of the wood splitting and you can punch them below the surface for a neat finish. For light work, and in some furniture making, panel pins are more suitable, and these too can be punched below the surface of your work to make a hidden fixing.

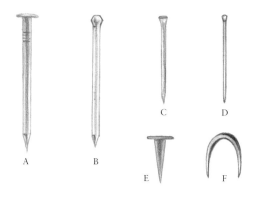

(A) ROUND WIRE NAIL, (B) OVAL NAIL, (C) LOST-HEAD NAIL, (D) PANEL PIN, (E) TACK OR STUD, (F) STAPLE

Always use a nail or pin of suitable length. Long pins tend to bend easily, so support them between your forefinger and thumb and take care when knocking them in. Short pins may be difficult to hold, so try pushing them through a piece of stiff card held between your finger and thumb.

Pins used in conjunction with glue can make quite a strong joint. Strength is improved, especially on wide boards, if "dovetail nailing" is used. To make any nailed assembly easier, tap the nail or pin almost through the top piece first, apply the glue, and then position the pieces of wood together and knock the nail or pin all the way in. When working with hardwoods, which tend to split easily, it is best to predrill holes slightly smaller than the nails or pins to be used. For a neat finish, punch the nails or pins below the surface of the wood using a small nail punch or nail set and hammer. The punch should have a concave tip to pre-

vent it slipping off the pin or nail head. Fill the holes left on the surface with a wood-filler or with a mixture of glue and sawdust.

Using screws Screws are used for joining pieces of wood together and for fitting hardware such as hinges, handles, and so on.

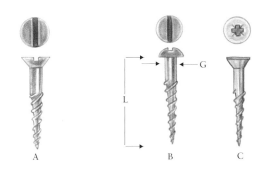

They are classified by length (L); the thickness of the shank, or gauge (G); and type of head. They are made in steel or brass and there are also several steel-coated varieties, such as chromium and zinc. The size is specified by length and the gauge by a number – the larger the number, the thicker the screw. Head types are basically either countersunk or flat head (A), designed to go flush with or below the surface of the wood; or round head (B), designed to sit on the surface. Screws may have the traditional straight slot for use with a conventional screwdriver, or be cross headed (C) for use with an appropriate cross-head screwdriver.

For most work in the projects section, countersunk, slotted steel screws are used. However, with oak you must always use brass screws to prevent the tannin in the wood corroding the screws.

Drilled holes are necessary when joining wood with screws, and when fitting hardware. With hardwoods, drill a clearance hole – one fractionally larger than the screw diameter – through the top piece, and a pilot hole – one smaller than the diameter of the screw threads – to the full length of the screw. In softwoods, the top clearance hole should be drilled, but you can use a bradawl

for making the pilot hole. Use a countersink to recess the surface or counterbore the top and fill the surface with a wooden plug if you intend to conceal the head completely. Make sure you use the correct size of screwdriver for the size of screw, and press down firmly on the screw head as it is turned to prevent damage to the slot. Soft steel screws are easily damaged.

Using adhesives Using an appropriate adhesive is often the most satisfactory way to join wood to wood, especially when it is used with one of the interlocking types of joint or when reinforced by nails or screws. For the glue to have maximum strength, you must first clean the parts that are to come into contact to remove any dust or loose wood that could create gaps – don't use glue as a space filler if you want a good joint. Then you must keep the pieces in tight contact until the glue is properly dry (see the manufacturer's recommendations), usually by cramping them together.

Plan the gluing-up stage of your work carefully. Have a clear, dust-free area in which to work and first of all test fit the pieces together (without using glue) to make sure that everything fits properly and is square. Have your glue and a damp cloth to hand; cramps should be ready and set to the right size with protective blocks available if needed. Use enough glue to prevent a dry joint but not so much that you create a messy clean-up job afterwards. Wipe away any surplus glue with a damp cloth. Bear in mind that glue marks can mar the appearance of some surface finishes.

MAKING JOINTS

Edge jointing When a wide piece of wood is called for, it may be necessary to join two narrower pieces together, edge to edge. The simplest and most satisfactory method is to use the plain rubbed joint. For this to work, you need to make sure that the mating edges are true and square along their entire length. You can avoid making the common error of planing more off the ends by planing the middle fractionally hollow. Planing the two edges at the same time helps accuracy. To test your results, hold the edges together and up to the light to identify any gaps.

When you are satisfied, apply glue to one of the adjoining edges, press the edges together, and rub them backward and forward a few times. This removes any air from the joint and rubs the glue into the fibres – which gives the joint its name.

To hold the edges in tight contact, a minimum of three sash or bar cramps are needed, placed as shown. Tighten the middle one first. Check your work for flatness, clean off any surplus glue, and leave it to dry overnight. Plane or, preferably, scrape the joint area clean if necessary afterwards.

The plain rubbed joint is fine for most work, but for larger surfaces, such as table tops, you can use a similar joint strengthened with dowels or by a loose tongue. To make a wider board, purchased tongue-and-groove boards can be glued together.

Grooves and rebates Although not strictly joints by themselves, grooves and rebates

form parts of joints. A groove is a narrow channel cut usually along the length of a component, and a rebate is a recess along an edge, either with or across the grain. Both may be used to hold panels in place. Special-purpose all-metal planes are available for making grooves and rebates. A rebate plane will only cut a rebate, while a plough plane will tackle rebates and grooves. There are various multiplanes that will also do both, and other work besides. When using these planes, make short cuts beginning at the far end of the work and finish off with light continuous cuts.

The portable electric router, fitted with interchangeable cutters, has now taken over the work once performed by these different hand tools. When it us used with a suitable guide fence or with a manufactured or custom-built routing table, the portable router is safe, accurate, and quick.

Housing joint This type of joint comprises a narrow trench or wide groove cut across the grain of a piece of wood into which the end of another piece, such as a shelf, is fitted. Housings may be full thickness (of the shelf) or bare-faced, meaning that the shelf thickness is reduced to fit a narrower housing, and they can be either made through or stopped, as shown. You can cut the joint entirely by hand, with a little help from a drilling machine if you like (see above, right), or you can use an electric router.

Full thickness
(stopped)

Bare-faced
(through)

Begin by measuring the thickness of the shelf (or the bare-faced tongue made on the end of the shelf) and set out the position of the shelves on the supporting side pieces. Make

the width of the housing joints fractionally less than the thickness of the shelves to ensure a tight fit. After checking, mark the cutting lines across the grain with a sharp marking knife. Gauge the depth of the joint – which is usually ⅓ the thickness of the side piece – from the inside face. Securely cramp the work to the bench. Using a sharp (¾in (19mm) chisel, cut into the knifed lines on the waste side to form a guide groove for the saw. Saw down to the depth of the housing joint and then chisel out the waste wood, working in toward the centre from both ends where possible (see above). You can use a drill to remove the bulk of the waste wood. Smooth the bottom of the joint and try the shelf for a fit. If necessary, plane a shaving off the underside of the shelf until you get a tight fit.

Where one piece of wood meets another at a corner, as, for example, in a box-like construction, you can use similar housing joints. If the housing is full thickness it becomes, in effect, a cross-grain rebate, and you should secure it with glue and nails. However, a bare-faced housing is preferable in most circumstances and, if well made, this joint is strong enough using glue alone.

Dovetail joints   You can obtain a much stronger corner joint using a dovetail joint, which is also particularly good for drawers. The strength of this joint lies in the increased gluing area and the interlocking shapes.

There are several types of dovetail, the simplest being the through dovetail. In this, the end-grain portions of the joint, the tails and pins (the bits in between the tail sockets), are visible on both sides. In the lapped dovetail, often used on drawer fronts, the end grain is concealed on one face.

In drawer construction, you always cut the tails on the side pieces. Cut the materials to the required length and square across the end. Number, or otherwise identify, the matching ends. For through dovetails, where the front and sides arc the same thickness of wood, mark out and cut the components as follows:

1. Set a marking (or cutting) gauge to the thickness of the wood and mark the ends of each piece all around – this is the depth line of the joint. Mark out the tails first, using either a T-bevel or a dovetail template. The tails should be evenly spaced and the marked positions squared across the end.

2. With the wood held upright in a vice, carefully saw on the waste side, using a dovetail or some other back saw, down to the depth line as shown above.

3. Remove the bulk of the waste wood using a coping saw and then finish removing the waste from both sides with a sharp bevel-edge chisel.

4. Mark out the sockets using the mating tails as a template. Hold the component to be marked upright in a vice and support the tail piece on it as shown. Align the tails carefully and mark clearly with a knife and square lines down to the depth line.

5. Cut away the waste wood as before, remembering to cut on the waste side of the marked lines, and clean out the joint with a sharp chisel. Test fit the joint and adjust as necessary with a chisel.

For lapped dovetails, the front piece is usually thicker than the sides – this extra thickness forms the lap that conceals the tails. Prepare your materials as described for through dovetails and, after deciding on the length of the tails (which are often equal to the thickness of the sides for convenience), set a marking gauge and mark the ends of the side pieces all around. Mark the front piece along the end and on the inside surfaces. Cut the tails and mark out the sockets as described for the through dovetail.

1. With the front piece held upright in a vice, carefully saw at an angle down to the gauged lines on the inside surface and lap. Remember to cut on the waste side of the lines.

2. With the piece secured flat on the bench, chisel out the waste wood beginning with vertical cuts (across the grain) and horizontal cuts. Use a sharp bevel-edge chisel and get right into the corners of the sockets. Test fit the joint and adjust as necessary.

You can cut dovetails by machine and these are usually recognizable by the even size and spacing of the pins and tails. Modern jigs, however, allow you to use a router to cut dovetails that are indistinguishable from hand-cut joints.

Cross-halving, or cross-lapped, joint   Where two pieces of wood (usually of the same thickness) are to cross each other at right angles, and you want the surfaces to remain flush, you will have to use a cross-halving, or cross-lapped, joint.

joint, only three are considered here: the stub, or blind, mortise and tenon; the haunched mortise and tenon; and the more specialized double mortise and tenon. The main parts of each of these joints are the mortise, which is a recess or slot cut into (usually) the upright member or stile, and the tenon, which is a reduced projection on the end of the mating piece (generally called the rail) made to fit tightly into the mortise.

Plane materials true and square, making sure that they are square across the ends. Where mortises come close to the end, it is usual practice to leave some extra length to the stiles initially to prevent the wood splitting. These projections are sawn off later.

1. Cut the rails to length, remembering to allow for the length of both tenons. Mark the required rail length and square all around with a sharp knife. This is the shoulder line of the tenon.

3. Cut the mortises first. If you are doing this by hand, it helps to drill vertically down between the marked lines with a smaller-sized drill to remove the bulk of the waste wood, and then use a chisel to clean and square the joint. Make mortises ⅛in (3mm) deeper than the length of the tenon.

Plane the materials to size and square and mark the position of the joint full width and square across each piece using a sharp knife. Also mark the lines squared down the sides in pencil. Set a marking gauge to half the thickness of the wood and mark in the depth of the joint equally on both pieces. Chisel a sloping groove into the knifed lines (on the waste side) to make a guide for the saw, and then saw vertically down to the gauged line indicating the depth of the joint. Chisel out the waste wood, working from both sides in so that it is smooth and flat.

Mortise and tenon joints The strongest as well as the most commonly used type of framing joint is the mortise and tenon. Although there are many variations of this

2. Mark out the positions of the mortises. The width required is the width of the tenons. Set the spurs of a mortise gauge to a chisel-width equal or close to a third the thickness of the rail. Use the gauge at this setting to mark the thickness of tenon all around and also to complete the marking of the mortise (see above).

4. Now cut the tenons. With the rail held in a vice, saw down both cheeks to the shoulder line, cutting on the waste side of the marked lines, with a tenon saw in three stages, as shown. Then, with the rail held to the bench, chisel a sloping groove into the knifed shoulder line, on the waste side, to make a guide for the saw. Saw vertically down to the previously made saw cut to remove the cheek waste. Finally, mark the reduction in tenon width and saw off the waste.

5. Trim the tenon to a good fit in the mortise. Aim to keep everything square so that the joints don't cause the frame to twist.

The haunched mortise and tenon is ideal when making a frame that is grooved to accept a panel, as in a door. The haunch can help to strengthen the joint, but here it also fits and fills the exposed end of the groove in the stile. Where possible, make the groove the same size as the mortise and cut out the mortise as previously described, after first cutting the groove. (See page 142.)

Mark out the tenon and saw down the cheeks, but mark off and retain the haunch portion when sawing off the remaining waste. Trim to fit.

Double tenons are used when joining wide rails to stiles where the long mortise required for a single, wide tenon would weaken the stile, or where a wide tenon might become loose through shrinkage. It is, for example, the correct joint to use when jointing large panelled doors and deep apron table frames. Mark out the joint as shown above. Cut the mortise, including the recess for the tenon haunch and central tongue, first. Then mark out and cut the double tenon, haunch, and tongue. Trim to fit.

There are machines for cutting mortises, as well as attachments that you can fit to a bench drill to do the same. Tenoning machines are used in commercial manufacture, but on a smaller scale, by using suitable jigs, you can cut tenons on a circular saw or band saw, or with a router.

Round tenons into drilled sockets This is the traditional joint often used in stool and chair making to join legs to seats or cross rails to uprights. Sockets can be either bored "through" or "blind"; through joints are often wedged (see below). Some woodworkers advocate tapered sockets, but straight, parallel-sided sockets give a more secure joint. First, bore out the required size of

Blind socket   Through-and-wedged socket

socket using a drill bit – the saw-toothed Forstner bit is most suitable – and then make the round tenon by whittling with a knife or rounding with cutting or abrasive tools. A general rule of thumb is that the socket depth should not be less than the socket diameter.

Draw boring (pegging joints) An old method of tightening up and securing mortise and tenon joints is to insert a wooden pin or peg through the joint. This is known as draw boring, and it is often incorrectly copied in some modern reproduction furniture by boring through the assembled joint and simply fitting a dowel.

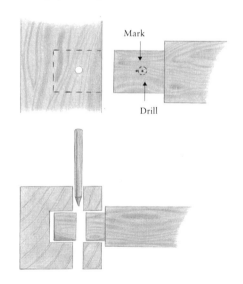

Mark

Drill

The correct way of making this joint is as follows. After you have cut the joint, but with the tenon withdrawn, bore a suitable hole through the side of the mortise. Then replace the tenon to its full depth and insert the drill again to just mark the surface of the tenon inside the mortise. Withdraw the tenon, re-mark it about $\frac{1}{16}$in (1.5mm) nearer to the shoulder and drill through at this point. The slight offset you have created will draw the joint up really tight when you drive the pin in. The pin should be straight grained and its head should be slightly larger than the hole and tapered to a point to ease starting. Cut the pin off flush on completion.

FINISHING

Some woods are more durable than others, but all will benefit from some kind of applied finish. Some finishes are designed to protect the surface by sealing the pores of the wood. Others, such as opaque paint, are used to obliterate or disguise the surface, while transparent polishes and varnishes serve to enhance and highlight the natural features of the wood. Additionally, finishes used on furniture act to give some resistance to the wear and tear of everyday use and abuse. Furthermore, many surface finishes can be renewed as time, and fashion, dictate.

Today there is a bewildering variety of wood-finishing materials. In earlier times, however, while there were several paint formulations and some oils and waxes, there was far less choice. For the country woodworker, choice was further limited by both cost and availability.

The subject of finishes is a complex one and here it is possible to make only general comments. Your local paint dealer should be able to advise you, and always read the manufacturers' labels on proprietary products before making your choice.

PAINT

The painted furniture and artefacts of Ancient Egypt and the evidence of the use of colour in medieval dwellings give us some clues to the early use of "paint". Locally available earth and vegetable pigments were used to colour a suitable medium, such as water (to make limewash and distemper), or combinations of water and other ingredients, such as linseed oil and egg yolk (to make tempera). Linseed oil was also used to make oil paints.

Milk paint Limewash and distemper proved less suitable for use on wood than on walls, and egg tempera and oil paint are expensive and time-consuming to make. In due course, a compromise product was found – milk paint. Milk paint is made by mixing earth pigments with skimmed milk and a little lime. In the rural communities of North America in particular, where its inexpensive ingredients were readily available and easy to prepare, milk paint became extremely popular. As well as being easy to apply, it dries to a durable, smooth, flat (matt) finish. Moreover, milk paint produces clear colours that mellow nicely with age.

You apply milk paint with a brush or sponge, and since it is water soluble it is pleasant to use and dries quite quickly, becoming lighter in colour as it does so. A second coat will increase the opacity of the finish. When the paint has dried, you can add a clear lacquer, glaze, or wax to seal and darken the surface. Milk paint is an authentic "old" paint finish, one that is also environmentally friendly. Modern water-soluble paints include a range of acrylics and emulsion paints.

Oil paint Oil-based paints were originally a mix of linseed oil, pigment, and white lead, with turpentine as a solvent. In modern formulations, oil-based paint is more likely to be a blend of oils and synthetic resins, with the lead omitted for safety and health reasons. The usual solvent is white spirit. Available in a very wide range of colours and three different finishes – matt, semigloss, and gloss – these paints are totally opaque and provide a reasonably tough and durable surface finish. With bare wood, however, you first need to apply a primer or undercoat. The disadvantages of oil paint are that it is slow to dry and brushes and so on have to be cleaned in white spirit.

VARNISHES

Traditional varnish is made from natural gums, such as copal, dissolved in oil (linseed) or spirit (methylated). This produces a product with a transparent, or near transparent, appearance that you can apply to prepared bare wood or over matt paint to act as a protective top coat. Varnish also acts as a preservative and as a means of obtaining a good, hardwearing surface finish.

Today, the most common type of "varnish" is polyurethane, available in matt, semigloss (satin), and gloss. Polyurethane gives a hard, durable finish and it also provides effective protection against moisture. It is best to brush on a number of thinned coats (diluted half and half by volume with white spirit) than one full-strength application straight from the tin. Allow each coat to dry thoroughly and rub back the surface of each coat (except the final top coat) with very fine abrasive paper. Be meticulous about removing dust, though, or the surface finish will be marred.

STAINS

Wood stains alter or enrich the colour of wood and enhance the natural figure, or grain pattern, of a piece of furniture. There are four general types: water stains, spirit stains, oil stains, and chemical stains. Never use any stain without first testing it.

Prepare the wood carefully before staining it. Surface blemishes and coarse grain will be emphasized by the stain, while patches of grease or adhesive will reject the treatment and leave an uneven finish.

Water stains penetrate the fibres of the wood, but in so doing they cause the grain to rise, making it necessary to sand the wood smooth before proceeding. Wetting the wood with water, allowing it to dry, and then sanding before staining reduces this problem. Oil stains do not cause the grain to rise, but they are slow drying and relatively expensive. Spirit-based stains are probably the most difficult to apply evenly due to their rapid drying time – dark patches where the stain overlaps can be a problem. Chemical stains work by reacting with the wood and the resulting colour can be unpredictable. After applying any stain, and after it has thoroughly dried, seal the surface of the wood with a varnish, oil, or wax.

WAX AND OIL

Beeswax and linseed oil are probably the oldest known surface finishes. Both are transparent, or nearly so, and both impart a wonderful lustre that brings out the best qualities of colour and grain. Readily available and quite easy to apply, both are popular and well liked. The disadvantages of both are that they offer comparatively little surface protection and are easily marred. But the virtue of these finishes is that they are easy to renew.

Wax There are several good polishes you can buy, but make sure the one you choose is based on beeswax – some use paraffin wax instead. Avoid polishes that contain silicon – these produce the much advertised "sparkle", but not much else in terms of protecting or nourishing the wood. All waxes are incompatible with other finishes.

You can apply a wax polish to bare wood and progressively build up the surface you want with additional applications. However, by giving the wood an initial application of a sealer, such as sanding sealer or a thinned coat of shellac or polyurethane, the wax will be more evenly distributed and you will save yourself a lot of work. Rub the sealer down with a very fine abrasive before waxing. Apply the wax with a soft cloth, rub it in well, and leave it to dry for a few minutes before buffing it with a clean, dry cloth. Subsequent applications of wax will improve the sheen and, in time, help to produce a rich patination.

Oil "Once a day for a week, once a week for a month, once a month for a year, and once a year forever" is an old adage about applying an oil finish. The traditional oil was linseed, and its use does indeed require numerous applications. Each must dry (by oxidization) before the next is applied, and the idea is to go on doing this until the wood can absorb no more oil.

Boiled linseed oil dries more quickly than the raw oil, but modern formulations, such as teak, tung, and Danish oils incorporating rapid oxidizing agents, are now more commonly used. You apply these proprietary oils in the same way as linseed, by brushing or on a cloth, but because they are more penetrating and quicker to dry, they require only two or three applications.

AGEING

There are various techniques you can use to simulate the effects of age, sunlight, dust, damp, and the general wear and tear of years of use. Known generally as "distressing" or "antiquing", these methods are now widely practised and accepted for their aesthetic appeal, although they are also used by fakers trying to pass modern-built furniture off as genuinely old. Distressing can involve doing actual damage to the wood, as well as using special finishes to simulate fading, peeling, crazing, patination, and similar effects.

DISTRESSING WOOD

Before applying any finish, you can artificially age wood by denting or scratching it, by scrubbing its surface with a wire brush, and by rounding over or purposely chipping corners and edges. Softwoods such as pine are especially suited to the wire-brush method. Wear on chair rails, table legs, and so on can easily be simulated by abrading these surfaces; for an authentic look, make sure that you apply this artificially induced damage where it would be most likely to occur in normal use.

A common method of further ageing new wood is to wipe it over with an antiquing glaze, made by mixing together small amounts of pigment such as burnt umber, raw sienna, or Vandyke brown in a transparent oil glaze. Make up a suitable glaze by mixing 1 part boiled linseed oil with 2 parts white spirit, or substitute thinned oil varnish or polyurethane. Alternatively, you can use a water-based glaze. Simply wipe or brush on this tinted glaze and then immediately wipe it off again, leaving pigment behind in the dents, hollows, and cracks.

Thinned grey or cream matt-finish paint brushed on and wiped off again will leave enough pigment behind in the grain of hardwoods to simulate age or a limewashed effect. Proprietary "old pine" stain will also convincingly age softwoods. Formulations containing lime, caustic soda, ammonia, or sulphuric acid can also be effective, but they are dangerous to use and you need to take extreme care.

Antique waxes – wax polish containing darkening pigments – applied to new wood will quickly give the appearance of a build-up of polish and dirt, which is what gives the patina of age. You can buy suitable wax polishes ready tinted or make them up yourself by adding pigments or shoe polish to ordinary wax furniture polish.

DISTRESSING PAINT

You can also apply antiquing glaze over a painted surface. This will darken the colour of the paint, producing an effect that would naturally take years to achieve. Rubbing a painted surface with abrasive paper or wire wool will lighten its colour, simulating both wear and tear and the effects of exposure to sunlight. Abrading the surface colour right off in places will allow underlying paint colours to show through in those areas. This can be a very effective technique, but you can also try applying a first coat of paint, allowing it to dry before applying a second one in a contrasting colour. Before this second coat has dried, rub it off in the areas that would normally receive the most wear to reveal the colour beneath (and perhaps, too, some areas of bare wood). It is very helpful to examine a real antique painted piece first to give you some ideas of how the end result should look.

Flaking paint is often a characteristic associated with old furniture, especially items that have been exposed to damp. Applying patches of wax, either to bare wood or a previously painted surface, will stop additional coats of paint adhering to those patches. When the top coat is dry, gently rub back the previously waxed areas to cause the paint to flake. Dampness may also cause painted surfaces to crack and craze. You can simulate this by using special "crackle" varnishes. This process makes use of the incompatibility and different drying times of oil-based and water-based varnishes. The best effects are achieved when two coats of contrasting base paints are used. If required, you can wipe more colour into the cracked surface after it has dried.

All distressing and antiquing processes require careful application if they are to be convincing. Bear in mind that wear would occur in some areas more than others, and that dust and dirt tends to accumulate in recesses such as deep mouldings. Also bear in mind that exposed surfaces, such as sharp edges, table tops, and drawer fronts, would tend to be lighter in colour due to wear and the fading effects of sunlight. Around door and drawer handles you would also find signs of wear and tear and a build-up of grime. Use artists' colours applied with a small brush to produce the desired effect.

Once you have achieved an aged appearance, apply a protective coat of varnish – but don't let it get too shiny.

WOOD GUIDE

It helps to know something of a wood's characteristics – its working properties, colour, durability, and so on – before choosing a particular type for a specific project. It also helps to know if it is botanically a hardwood (H) or a softwood (S). Below, you will find a brief guide to those North American and European timbers that have been used or recommended for the projects contained in this book and that are easily available to the country woodworker.

You can readily purchase prepared wood from timber yards and other retail outlets (see Directory, pages 156-7). Softwoods are generally less expensive to buy than hardwoods, but are also less durable. In some countries, large quantities of wood, both hardwoods and softwoods, are sold by volume – i.e. by the cubic foot. This is a quantity of wood equal to a board 1in thick x 12in wide x 12ft long (25mm x 305mm x 3.6m). For smaller quantities of wood, it is more usual to be quoted a price per piece or per foot (meter) for a given, measured section. The standard measurement in America is the board foot, which is equal to a board 1in thick x 12in square (25mm x 305mm square).

Ash (H)

The European ash (*Fraxinus excelsior*) is a large tree whose common name generally reflects its country of origin. In Canada and the United States, the ash (*F. americana*) is generally a little smaller, but there are many varieties, such as black, white, yellow, and blue ash. It has a coarse but usually straight grain and is characterized by its strength and resilience. It is whitish to light brown in colour, has a distinctive figure (grain pattern), is easy to work, and takes a good polish. It is not durable outdoors, however, unless it is treated with a suitable preservative.

Beech (H)

This strong, hardwearing wood has good working properties. The European beech (*Fagus sylvatica*) grows into a large tree and is favoured for its fine, uniform texture. The American beech (*F. grandifolia*) is a relatively small tree but with similar strength and working properties to its European counterpart, although it does have a slightly coarser texture. Beech is generally pale to reddish brown in colour, and although its figure often lacks character, it stains and polishes well. It requires treatment with a preservative if you intend to use it in damp conditions.

Birch (H)

This is probably the world's hardiest and most-widespread tree. Birch (*Betula sp.*) varies from invasive scrub to moderate-sized trees. The characteristic birch of North America is the paper birch (*B. papyrifera*), while sweet birch (*B. lenta*) and yellow birch (*B. alleghanensis*) are also common. In Britain, the silver birch (*B. pendula*) and *B. pubescens* are common. Birch has a creamy white sap wood and pale brown heartwood. It works and finishes reasonably well but it is not durable when used outdoors.

Cedar (S)

The true cedar, cedar of Lebanon (*Cedrus libani*), is a large tree with a trunk up to 5ft (1.5m) in diameter. Its wood is straight grained if a little brittle, but it is easy to work (except around any knots). The cedar has an aromatic wood whose scent discourages moths. American "cedars" include white cedar (*Thuja occidentalis*), western red cedar (*T. plicata*), yellow cedar (*Chamaecyparis nootkatensis*), and others. Both the white and western red cedar are reddish brown in colour and slightly coarse grained, and western red cedar splits easily. Yellow cedar is fine textured, easily worked, and pale yellow in colour.

Cherry (H)

American cherry, also known as black cherry (*Prunus serotina*), is a good, decorative wood, fine textured and straight grained. It makes a tree of moderate size, although there are smaller varieties such as the pin and sweet cherries. The European cherry (*P. avium*) is also a small tree and its wood is mainly used only for small-scale work. Cherry wood, which is reddish brown in colour, is not difficult to work if your tools are sharp. It finishes well and takes a high polish.

Elm (H)

Once common in parts of North America and Britain, elm – including *Ulmus americana* and *U. procera*, the American and English elms, respectively – is fast disappearing due to the ravages of Dutch elm disease. Larger in size in Britain than in America, elm trees produce wood that is coarse textured and often cross grained, but it works well when sharp tools are used. Its colour is beige-brown and most varieties and hybrids have an attractive figure, especially *U. procera*. It is not naturally durable when used outdoors.

Hazel (H)

More of a shrub than a tree, the European hazel (*Corylus avellana*) is widespread throughout much of Britain where, in the past, it was extensively grown as coppice. It produces strong, straight sticks for a variety of craft applications. Native American hazels include *C. americana* and *C. californica*.

Hickory (H)

Native to Canada and eastern parts of America, hickory (*Carya glabra*, *C. laciniosa*, among others) is a strong, straight-grained wood similar in appearance and main characteristics to ash. Its fibrous wood is tougher than that of ash, however.

Lime (H)

A fine-textured wood, lime (*Tilia vulgaris*), also known as linden, is easily worked and, because it cuts evenly in all directions, it is excellent when you want a wood for carving. It has a creamy white coloured wood. The American lime (*T. americana*) is known as Basswood – the name that is also given to the wood of the tulip tree.

Maple (H)

Of the many maples, sugar maple (*Acer saccharum*), also known as hard or rock maple, is perhaps best known throughout North America. It is a heavy, hard wood with a close-textured grain, white to pale brown in colour. It can sometimes be difficult to work, but it is hard wearing and finishes well. Red maple (*A. rubrum*) is not as hard or strong as *Acer saccharum*, but it is easier to work. In Britain, the field maple (*A. campestre*) is generally little more than a small hedgerow tree of limited commercial value. None of the maples is naturally durable when used outdoors.

Oak (H)

There are many different oaks. American varieties are generally grouped as white oak (*Quercus alba*) and red oak (*Q. rubra*), while the two varieties native to Britain are the common, or European, oak (*Q. robur*) and the sessile oak (*Q. petraea*). Oak wood is renowned for its strength and durability, but these qualities vary according to growing conditions and growth rates. All are hard and durable and work well. White oak has similar characteristics to the European varieties, while red oak is coarser grained and has a less attractive figure. Colour varies from pale yellow to brown, often with a pinkish tint. Oak wood contains tannic acid, which corrodes ferrous metals.

Pine (S)

This wood is probably used more than any other. Pine is the general name given to all members of the *Pinus* family – and, commercially, to several others that are not. The character of the 35 or so varieties of American pine varies geographically from the hard, pitch pines of the south (*P. palustris*) to the softer pines such as Weymouth or yellow pine (*P. strobus*) of the east and the western white pine (*P. monticola*). Yellow pine is an easily worked wood, pale yellow to brown in colour, while western white pine is similar in appearance but tougher. In Europe, Scots pine (*P. sylvestris*), especially, provides the popular red deal or redwood, which is a relatively strong, slightly resinous wood, yellow-brown to red-brown in colour, often with a distinctive figure. It works easily and well (except around the knots), and can be brought to a good finish. All the varieties of pines take stain, paint, and polish well. None is durable outdoors,' however, unless first treated with a suitable preservative.

Sycamore (H)

American and British sycamores are unrelated trees – the former belong to the plane family (*Platanus occidentalis*), while the latter are maples (*Acer pseudoplatanus*), the false plane. The American sycamore is an even-textured wood, pale reddish brown in colour. It is easy to work and polishes well. The British sycamore also has an even texture, but it is finer textured than its American equivalent, and is white to creamy white in colour. It works and finishes well, coming to a lustrous surface. Neither species is durable if used outdoors, however.

Walnut (H)

This is a distinctive wood with some excellent characteristics. American black walnut (*Juglans nigra*) is a large tree. It has a tough, rather coarse-textured wood, with both straight and wavy grain. Its heartwood is rich purple brown to black in colour. It works well, takes a high polish, and is moderately durable outdoors. European walnut (*J. regia*) is a smaller tree, and its wood varies in colour from grey brown to brown, often with darker streaks. Its characteristics and working properties are similar to *J. nigra*.

TEMPLATES

The template patterns on pages 150–5 have been grouped together by design project (see key). To save space, the patterns overlap, but you can easily differentiate between the pieces by looking for the identifying letters found inside a coded bubble along one of the edges. Make a separate tracing for each pattern piece, making sure that you label each one with the appropriate letter. The templates on pages 150–4 are full size; those on page 155 have been reduced in size with each grid square representing 1 inch.

DIRECTORY OF SUPPLIERS

Note: while every effort has been made to ensure that the following details are accurate and up to date, these details may vary from time to time.

WOOD AND TOOLS

British Gates & Timber Ltd
Biddenden
Ashford
Kent
TW27 8DD
Wood, tools, accessories.

Craft Supplies
The Mill
Millers Dale
Buxton
Derbyshire
SK17 8SN
Wood, tools, accessories, finishing supplies.

Fine Wood & Tool Store
Riverside Sawmills
Boroughbridge
North Yorkshire
YO5 9LU
Hardwoods, tools, books, finishing supplies.

Limehouse Timber Ltd
18 Robert Leonard Industrial Estate
Stock Road
Southend-on-Sea
Essex
SS2 5QD
Native & imported hardwoods.

Milland Fine Timber
The Working Tree
Milland
Hampshire GU30 7JS
Native & sustainable source imported hardwoods, tools, books.

West & Sons Ltd
Salham
Petworth
West Sussex GU28 0PU
Native & imported hardwoods & softwoods.

Yandle & Sons Ltd
Hurst Works
Martock
Somerset TA12 6JU
Wood, tools, accessories.

PAINTS AND FINISHES

Craig & Rose plc
172 Leith Walk
Edinburgh EH6 5EP
Traditional varnishes.

Farrow & Ball Ltd
33 Uddens Trading Estate
Wimborne
Dorset BH21 7NL
Traditional paints.

Heart of the Country
Home Farm
Swinsen
Nr Litchefield
Staffordshire S14 9QR
American traditional paints.

House of Harbru
Unit 3 Cuba Industrial Estate
Boolton Road North
Ramsbottom BL0 0NE
Wax polish, oils, stains.

Liberon
Mountfield Industrial Estate
New Romney
Kent TN28 8XU
Wax polishes & other finishing products.

Pine Brush Products
Stockingate
Oton Clanford
Staffordshire ST18 9PB
Milk paint & other finishing products, brushes.

Rustins Ltd
Waterloo Road
London NW2 7TX
Finishing & restoration products.

MISCELLANEOUS

Jacobs, Young & Westbury
Bridge Road
Haywards Heath
West Sussex RH16 1UA
Seat weaving materials, rush cane & cord.

H.E. Savill
9 St Martin's Place
Scarborough
North Yorkshire Y011 2QH
Period furniture fittings.

Shaker Shop
25 Harcourt Street
London W1
Shaker furniture, pegs, kits, seating tape.

Woodfit Ltd
Chorley
Lancashire
PR6 7EA
Traditional & modern furniture hardware.

PLACES OF INTEREST

BRITAIN

American Museum in Britain
Claverton Manor
Bath
Avon
BA2 7BT
Colonial & Shaker interiors, furniture & artefacts.

Highland Folk Museum
Duke Street
Kingussie
Scotland
Early local furniture & artefacts.

Museum of Lakeland Life & Industry
Abbot Hall
Kendal
Cumbria
Trade workshops & period interiors, furniture & artefacts, tools, etc.

Norfolk Rural Life Museum
Grassenhall
East Dereham
Norfolk
Labourers' cottage & artefacts.

Welsh Folk Museum
St Fagins
Cardiff CF5 6XB
*Furnished period cottages,
rural artefacts, tools.*

NORTH AMERICA

Adirondack Museum
Blue Mountain Lake
NY 12812
Regional crafts & furniture.

Colonial Williamsburg
PO Box C
Williamsburg VA 23187
*Early Colonial interiors,
furniture & artefacts.*

Hancock Shaker Village
Albany Road, Route 20
PO Box 898
Pittsfield MA 02102
*Shaker interiors, furniture,
artefacts, etc.*

Metropolitan Museum of Art
Fifth Avenue at 82nd Street
NY 10028
*Rare, early furniture &
artefacts.*

Old Sturbridge Village
1 Old Sturbridge Village Road
Sturbridge
MA 015662
*Colonial-period furniture &
artefacts.*

WOODWORKING COURSES

Jack Hill Workshops
PO Box 20
Midhurst
West Sussex
GU29 0JD
*Country furniture, chair
making & rural crafts,
accessories, etc.*

Chris Mowe
Stockingate
Coton Clanford
Staffordshire
ST18 9PB
Antique paint finishing.

West Dean College
Chichester
West Sussex
PO18 0QZ
*Furniture making, chair seat
weaving, finishing.*

BIBLIOGRAPHY

Gilborn, Craig. *Adirondack Furniture and the Rustic Tradition.*
Abrams Inc., New York. 1987.

Hill, Jack. *Country Chair Making.*
David & Charles, Newton Abbot. 1993.

Kettell, Russell H. *The Pine Furniture of Early New England.*
Dover, New York. 1949.

Kinmonth, Claudia. *Irish Country Furniture.*
Yale University Press. 1993.

Knell, David. *England Country Furniture.*
Berry & Jenkins, London. 1992.

Mack, Daniel. *Making Rustic Furniture.*
Sterling Lark, New York. 1992.

Miller, Judith & Martin. *Period Finishes and Effects.*
Mitchell Beazley, London. 1992.

Shea, John G. *Antique Country Furniture of North America.*
Van Nostrand Reinhold, New York. 1975.

Sparkes, Ivan. *English Domestic Furniture.*
Spurbooks, Bourne End. 1980.

Sprigg, J. & Larkin, D. *Shaker: Life, Work, and Art.*
Cassell, London. 1988.

INDEX

ACKNOWLEDGEMENTS

I thank Judith More for asking me to write this book and for her support throughout, Sophie Pearse who was in at its birth, and Jenny Jones who saw it through its final, sometimes fraught, stages. Thanks to the Art Department and Production, and those background sub-editors, readers and illustrators who, bit by bit, helped us to put it all together. Thanks also to the Accounts Department, whose literary contribution – writing advance cheques – should not be overlooked.

Thanks to James Merrell for his superb photography; my American friends Merryll and Ed Saylan, who read part of the manuscript; Chris Mowe and Henryk Terpilowski for advice and help with the antique finishing; and Linda Fielder for word processing, again.

Finally, I would like to thank all those who, over the years, have taught me to love and understand wood and how to make useful things with it. And I thank God for the trees we all use.

The publishers would like to thank the following for kindly allowing us to photograph their homes:
Shirley Dupree, Fran Sansom & Jack Hill, Howard Kaplan, Tasha and Jack Polizzi, George Schmidt, Maryanne Wilkins

Antique and modern country-style furniture similar to that seen in the photographs can be obtained at:
Makers 1 Ives Street, off Draycott Avenue, London SW3 2ND, England
T.P. Saddle Blanket & Trading 304 Main Street, Great Barrington MA, USA
Howard Kaplan Antiques 827 Broadway, New York NY 10003, USA
Howard Kaplan Bath 47 East 12th Street, New York NY 10003, USA

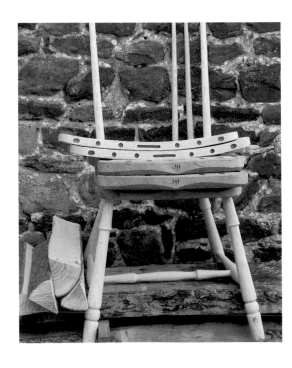